Praise for *LeBron's Dream Team*
by LeBron James and Buzz Bissinger

"Compelling . . . An uplifting tale of bonding, of a handful of friends who grow as tight as brothers as they get squeezed by pressure, expectations and even racism. It's hard not to root for the group, and it's gratifying when their hard work and loyalty to each other leads to a happy ending." —Associated Press

"The most high-powered pairing. LeBron. Buzz. The mononymous stars in their respective fields—basketball's James, sports books' Bissinger—teamed up on [*LeBron's Dream Team*] . . . an entertaining, well-written reminder that even if he seems to have been around forever, James didn't go directly from the nursery to the NBA." —*Sports Illustrated*

"[James] was smart to hook up with Mr. Bissinger, who showed in *Friday Night Lights* that he writes about young men and sports as well as anyone alive." —*The New York Times*

"Exhaustively detailed, enhanced by James' maturity and candor from six years' remove, and Bissinger's well-crafted writing providing context . . . an interesting and worthwhile read." —Dan McGrath, *Chicago Tribune*

"You'll learn a lot about [James] and his hard times as the son of a single, working-class mother, but what distinguishes the memoir is how James turns the spotlight on his teammates. James got all the attention as the star player for St. Vincent-St. Mary High School, and [*LeBron's Dream Team*] is his way of giving thanks to the supporting cast." —*Newsday*

"More about friendship than it is about fame, more about loyalty and hope than it is about the millions James has earned in a few short years as an NBA standout." —Julia Keller, *Chicago Tribune*

"This is a coming-of-age tale, approached from a different angle, and deftly done. The reportage is thorough to a fare-thee-well, what you would expect from a seasoned veteran, and their overall collaboration makes for an engaging read." —*The Philadelphia Inquirer*

"For the ordinary reader, [*LeBron's Dream Team*] also delivers an emotional wallop. The book can be read as a variation on the themes of masculinity, as a young LeBron and his buddies try out different approaches."   —*The Cleveland Plain Dealer*

"A poignant memoir chronicling [LeBron's] formative years and coming of age in Akron, Ohio . . . A compelling autobiography illustrating the evolution of LeBron into a selfless role model worthy of emulation."
—Newsblaze.com

"An excellent read."   —Hoopsworld.com

"The coauthors dramatically re-create the minute-by-minute highlights of key games in St.V's national-championship drive, but they also interject some serious social commentary on the vindictiveness, greed and exploitation that can infect the seemingly pristine world of amateur sports. . . . A simple but moving story about the double-edged sword of precocious athletic talent and the redemptive power of teamwork."
—*Kirkus Reviews*

"A warm, thoughtful memoir by a young man who, one imagines, will never forget his humble origins."   —*Booklist*

"When I first saw LeBron James play as a professional, it was his selflessness that dazzled me the most. After reading [*LeBron's Dream Team*], I now understand why. It is a book of five boys coming together to learn the true meaning of teamwork and togetherness, loyalty and love, through highs and lows and thick and thin. It is a book filled with excitement and unforgettable characters. It is a book that will incredibly move and inspire you."   —Jay-Z

"Our sense of modern athletes is often limited to what highlight reels and marketing campaigns reveal or obscure. [*LeBron's Dream Team*] is the compelling and often poignant story of a remarkable group of young men only one of whom happens to be a future NBA superstar. In the end we care about them all, even as we come away with a truer understanding and appreciation of the circumstances and relationships that forged one of the most significant sports figures of our time."
—Bob Costas, NBC sports commentator

"In the Olympics, LeBron was a star, a leader, and the ultimate teammate. He helped our team become a family. Reading [*LeBron's Dream Team*] taught me how he became that kind of a teammate, developing the selflessness and loyalty that define who he is. What an amazing story." —Mike Krzyzewski, Duke University men's basketball coach and the Gold Medal–winning coach of the U.S. men's basketball team, 2008 Olympics

"Reading about LeBron James' transition from boyhood to manhood was a thrill for me. [*LeBron's Dream Team*] is a remarkable and riveting story, filled with lessons of life we can all learn from."
—Warren Buffett

"The clock ticks, the suspense tightens, the scrappy kids from hard-luck Akron leave you hanging on every shot. But the wonder of [*LeBron's Dream Team*] is that it's hardly about basketball. Instead it is a nuanced coming-of-age drama about American culture and race, about organized sports as redeemer and exploiter, and about the blessing and curse of celebrity. At this book's heart, though, is an uncommon bond forged in youthful innocence and desire, a friendship at least as meaningful as anything LeBron James will ever add to his trophy case."
—Steve Lopez, author of *The Soloist*

"Told in a voice that is streetwise, yet gentle, [*LeBron's Dream Team*] shows how inner determination trumps bad breaks and how a winning combination of coaches, mentors, and friends turns lucky breaks into a way of life. If a book can have game, this one does."
—Madeleine Blais, author of *In These Girls, Hope Is a Muscle*

ABOUT THE AUTHOR

LeBron James plays for the NBA'S Cleveland Cavaliers. His superstardom is hard to overstate: at seventeen he was featured on the cover of *Sports Illustrated*; at nineteen he became the youngest rookie of the year in NBA history; at twenty-three he was named the third highest paid athlete in the world (including endorsements), after Tiger Woods and David Beckham. In 2006–7 he led the Cavaliers to their first NBA finals ever and finished second place in the vote for the league's most valuable player. In 2007–8 he became the youngest player in NBA history to score 10,000 points and topped the league in scoring. He was a key member of the U.S. men's basketball team that won a Gold Medal in the 2008 Olympics. The Cavaliers finished the 2008–9 season with the best record in the NBA. They lost the Eastern Conference finals to the Orlando Magic, in which James scored 40 or more points in three of six games. He was also named the league's most valuable player by a landslide. He is only the third man (and the first African American man) to appear on the cover of *Vogue*. He has hosted *Saturday Night Live*, graced Oprah's stage, and appeared on the cover of *Fortune*.

Pulitzer Prize–winner Buzz Bissinger wrote the American classic *Friday Night Lights*, which was named the fourth best book on sports ever by *Sports Illustrated* and the best on football. It was also named the best sports book of the past twenty-five years by ESPN. That work, about high school football in the town of Odessa, Texas, has sold close to two million copies to date and spawned a film and TV series. His other books include *A Prayer for the City* and the *New York Times* bestseller *Three Nights in August*. He is a contributing writer for *Vanity Fair*.

LeBron's Dream Team

How Five Friends
Made History

LeBRON JAMES

and

BUZZ BISSINGER

PENGUIN BOOKS

Previously published as *Shooting Stars*

PENGUIN BOOKS
Published by the Penguin Group
Penguin Group (USA) Inc., 375 Hudson Street, New York, New York 10014, U.S.A. • Penguin
Group (Canada), 90 Eglinton Avenue East, Suite 700, Toronto, Ontario, Canada M4P 2Y3
(a division of Pearson Penguin Canada Inc.) • Penguin Books Ltd, 80 Strand, London WC2R
0RL, England • Penguin Ireland, 25 St Stephen's Green, Dublin 2, Ireland (a division of Penguin
Books Ltd) • Penguin Group (Australia), 250 Camberwell Road, Camberwell, Victoria 3124,
Australia (a division of Pearson Australia Group Pty Ltd) • Penguin Books India Pvt Ltd, 11
Community Centre, Panchsheel Park, New Delhi – 110 017, India • Penguin Group (NZ),
67 Apollo Drive, Rosedale, North Shore 0632, New Zealand (a division of Pearson
New Zealand Ltd) • Penguin Books (South Africa) (Pty) Ltd, 24 Sturdee Avenue,
Rosebank, Johannesburg 2196, South Africa

Penguin Books Ltd, Registered Offices:
80 Strand, London WC2R 0RL, England

First published in the United States of America as *Shooting Stars* by The Penguin Press,
a member of Penguin Group (USA) Inc. 2009
Published in Penguin Books 2010

9 10

THE LIBRARY OF CONGRESS HAS CATALOGED THE HARDCOVER EDITION AS FOLLOWS:
James, LeBron.
Shooting stars / LeBron James and Buzz Bissinger.
p. cm.
ISBN 978-1-59420-232-2 (hc.)
ISBN 978-0-14-311822-0 (pbk.)
1. James, LeBron. 2. Basketball players—United States—Biography. I. Bissinger, H. G. II. Title.
GV994.J36J36 2009
796.323092—dc22   [B]   2009016067

Printed in the United States of America
DESIGNED BY AMANDA DEWEY

Penguin is committed to publishing works of quality and integrity.
In that spirit, we are proud to offer this book to our readers;
however, the story, the experiences, and the words
are the author's alone.

To my mother, without whom
I would not be where I am today

LEBRON

We all we got.

—SIAN COTTON

Contents

LeBron's Dream Team

Prologue

I am a sophomore at St. Vincent–St. Mary, a coed Catholic high school on North Maple Street overlooking the small cluster of downtown Akron. It has fine academics, and it's about three miles from where I live, with my mother on the sixth floor of a brooding apartment building on the crest of a small hill. I have my own room that I have decorated with posters of my favorite NBA players—Michael Jordan, Kobe Bryant, Allen Iverson. I would like to say I go to St. Vincent for the fine academics, but that would not be true. I go there to play basketball with three friends who have become my brothers, Little Dru and Sian and Willie.

We have a coach who is driven and maniacal and seems a little bit crazy sometimes. He spits out obscenities whenever we do something wrong in practice. "That was fucking terrible" is one of his favorite phrases. He is only five-eight, and for those of us who are tall, he never reaches eye level when he yells, no matter how much he stretches. But he is also brilliant. He criticizes me mercilessly, as if I have no idea of what I am doing, but he does it because he is convinced I can play in the NBA someday. He calls Sian, who is big and burly and menacing, a "coward" because he knows it is a way of motivating and challenging him. He is maybe a little bit softer on Little Dru, probably because he identifies with him. Little Dru plays with a huge rock on his shoulder since he is only five-three, and that's giving him every benefit of the doubt. Our coach guides us with the same rock on his shoulder, given his family legacy and his own professional disgrace when he was younger. He knows that Willie has come back from shoulder surgery the previous summer, and he realizes that the road back to the player he once was has been long and difficult, a promise that is no longer promising. That still doesn't stop him from cursing and swearing and getting frustrated and treating us like the college players he once coached instead of the high school players we actually are.

We are doing well as sophomores. More and more, we are playing with the warrior mentality that he has been trying to instill in us. More and more, we are making fewer and fewer mistakes. He is preparing us for something, and then we figure out what it is, the biggest game of our lives against the greatest dynasty in all of high school sports, Oak Hill Academy. It is a prep school in a town called Mouth of Wilson, Virginia, tucked into the western triangle of the state near Bridle Creek and Volney and dozens of other little dots on the map. Its players include such NBA stalwarts as Jerry Stackhouse, Kevin Durant, and Rod Strickland, plus over a hundred players who have gone to play basketball at the Division I level. Fourteen of its players have become NBA draft picks, including six in the first round. And here we are playing them, a bunch of upstart kids from Akron.

WE HAVE NO CHANCE against the lineup they put out on the court, maybe one of the best lineups ever in the history of high school basketball. Their center, DeSagana Diop from Senegal, is seven-one and 305 pounds and is sure to be a first-round draft pick. Their shooting guard, high school All-American Rashaad Carruth, has already committed to the University of Kentucky. Their point guard, high school All-American Billy Edelin, has committed to Syracuse University. Rounding out the middle at six-seven and close to 300 pounds is Mario Boggan, who will end up at Oklahoma State. Our hope and prayer is to make it respectable.

SOMEHOW, Sian holds down the middle and prevents Diop from going wild (he is kept to 15). Little Dru, despite his diminutive size, has willed himself into a 3-point shooter. Willie comes off the bench with spark and bite. We also have another player named Romeo. He is a selfish, self-absorbed, self-centered pain in the ass we mostly want to strangle. He is so out of shape he only plays in the second half. But he is six-six and has a commanding presence inside when he awakens from his lethargy, and he has awakened today. We are making it close. We even lead by a point at the end of the first quarter, 19–18, and by 6 at halftime, 42–36.

In the early minutes of the third quarter we build our lead to 10, 52–42. Yet it is only a matter of time. How can you stop a backcourt that features Rashaad Carruth and Billy Edelin? You can't. By the end of the third quarter Oak Hill holds a 2-point lead, 62–60. They are poised to pull away like they always do. At least St. V, as we call the school, will feel no shame. We stayed neck and neck for three quarters. We fought harder than they ever expected.

Then it gets hot.

The lead changes eight times in the final quarter. St. V pulls ahead by a point with 1:50 left, 78–77. I am playing well, with 21 points in the first half and 33 at that point. It is in our grasp. We can feel it.

There is 1:35 left to play when Billy Edelin, who is 12 for 12 during the game, hits a layup to give Oak Hill a 1-point lead, 79–78. But we get the ball back. There is one final shot left. Little Dru has gone 5 for 5 beyond the 3-point arc. His hand is hot. But the ball is mine, because it has to be mine.

The buzzer is about to sound. I take a running jumper. I experience the sensation of everything going into slow motion as I watch the ball go into the rim. And bounce around forever and ever.

And roll out as time disappears.

People who watched me that day tell me I played a great game. Maybe I deserve the compliment. Maybe I don't, because when it counts, when the game is there to be won or lost, I missed. I let my brothers Little Dru and Sian and Willie down. We are in search of a dream that goes beyond defeating Oak Hill. It is a dream that goes back to when we were kids who didn't know any better, and it fell away from that rim with the taunting cruelty that is basketball.

I cry afterward. I don't know what else to do. In the mix of those tears, I can't stop wondering, Will we ever get the chance again to realize that dream, or is a dream exactly that, just a dream? I do not know.

1.

Mapmakers

I rode my bike all over Akron when I was small, going here, going there, just trying to stay out of trouble, just trying to keep busy, just really hoping the chain wouldn't break like it sometimes did. If you went high up on North Hill in the 1980s, you could tell that life was not like it once was: the obsolete smokestacks in the distance, the downtown that felt so tired and weary. I won't deny it—there was something painful about all of that. It got to me, this place in north-eastern Ohio that had once been so mighty (at one point it was the fastest-growing city in the country) but was mighty no more. This place that was struggling to be something again.

It was still my hometown. The more I rode my bike around, and you could ride just about everywhere because it was midwestern small and compact, the more familiar I became with it. I rode along Copley Road, the main thoroughfare of West Akron, past the dark of redbrick apartment buildings with red-trimmed windows. A little bit farther up, I went past the Laundry King and Queen Beauty Supply. Riding along East Avenue, which took you from the western part of the city into the south, I went past modest two-story homes with porches and the brown concrete of the Ed Davis Community Center.

I descended into the valley of South Akron along Thornton Street, past the blond brick of Roush's Market and the Stewart & Calhoun Funeral Home. South Akron was a tough neighborhood, but still I rode, past Akron Automatic Screw Products and the aluminum siding of the Thornton Terrace apartments. Along Johnston Street I went into the east side, past simple homes of red and green and blue that looked like a rainbow. I turned south on Arlington, past the Arlington Church of God and Bethel Baptist and Allied Auto. I came to the Goodyear clock tower, towering high like the Washington Monument and the great symbol of what Akron had once been, the "Rubber Capital of the World," producing tires by the millions until all the great factories closed.

I biked up the north side into a section of the city known as the Bottom and went past the Elizabeth Park projects—my own home for a time—two-story apartment buildings in unsmiling rows, some of which had been condemned, some of which had been boarded up, some that had screen doors with the hinges torn off or the wire mesh stripped away. I headed back west and biked along Portage Path, a wealthy section of town with sprawling houses of brick and stone and shiny black shutters all perfectly aligned.

I knew I would never live there unless some miracle happened, something fell from the sky, a shooting star that landed on top of me and my mom and made our lives better and carried us up from the projects. But that wasn't the Akron I thought of anyway. Much of it was taken up by the neighborhoods that I went past on my bike, humble homes with tiny tufts of lawn that people tended and took care of. Because even in my darkest days growing up, and there were some dark ones, ones that left me up half the night scared and lonely and worried, that's what Akron always meant to me—people taking care of things, people taking care of each other, people who found you and protected you and treated you like their own son even when you weren't. With a population of about 225,000 when I was growing up, it was still small enough to feel intimate, a place you could put your arms around, a place that would put its arms around you.

There was something wholesome about it, the best of the Midwest, Cleveland without the 'hoods where you could go in and never come back out. One of my favorite spots in town was Swensons, which, straight out of *Happy Days*, still served up a burger and fries and Cherry Coke on a tray that was attached to the window of your car by a goofy-looking teenager still dealing with acne. I loved those burgers at Swensons, loved the scene and the smell and best of all the taste (order it with everything to get the full effect). But it wasn't until much later, when I was blessed with a skill I was able to develop, that I ever got much of a chance to eat one. A burger at Swensons? There was no way I could afford something like that.

Because Akron, for all its goodness of heart, wasn't soft. There were gangs and there were drugs and there were grim housing projects where sirens and gunfire went off in the night. There was an inner-city, maybe not as bad as Cleveland or Chicago or Philadelphia. But it was there, and I know it was there because I spent a lot of my childhood living within it, hearing those sounds and just trying to keep going, just keep my head low and keep on moving. And maybe if there was anything that was really different about me from other kids growing up in similar circumstances, it was that idea:

Just keep on moving.

Growing up in the inner city is not the hardest thing in the world to do. What my mom Gloria went through—having me by herself when she was sixteen years old and trying to raise me and give me everything I wanted—was so much harder. But certainly it's also not the easiest place in the world to begin your life, particularly when you see so many people who never even get to the middle.

You definitely have no choice but to see and hear things you never want to experience and you never ever want your kids to experience— violence and drug abuse and the mournful music of those police sirens wailing. You lie in bed, and you just know something bad is happening, something heavy, and you just thank the Lord that it isn't you out there in it, and you lie in bed some more and just wait for those sounds to go away. Eventually they do. But it's hard to fall back asleep after that. Sometimes it's impossible. Was there just a terrible fight? Are the police busting for drugs again? What was that noise? No matter how much I tried to shut everything out, and I have always been good at shutting everything out, they have an impact. But maybe not the way you might be thinking.

Because it helps you grow up when you are an only child. It helps you to learn to take care of yourself. It also helps to motivate you—if you ever are lucky enough to find a way out of where you are, even if it's for a few hours, you are going to run with it as fast as you can.

Whatever I went through, I always loved Akron. Even back then, growing up in the 1980s and 1990s, there was one thing that always bothered me. In school, whenever I looked at a map of the United States—because you know how schools are, there is always a map of the United States in every classroom—the first thing I did was look at Ohio. There was Cleveland, of course, because everybody knew Cleveland, former home of the legendary Browns and Jimmy Brown, home of the Indians. On some maps there might be the state capital of Columbus. Or even Cincinnati. But where was Akron? How come there was never Akron?

Akron who? Akron where?

Akron nobody, as far as the mapmakers were concerned. That always got to me. Why wasn't my hometown there? I don't remember how old I was exactly, maybe eight or nine. But I promised myself, in the funny way that little kids make promises over things that nobody else in the world cares about, that one day I was going to put Akron on the map. Maybe not literally, because you could tell those mapmakers were a prickly bunch, but I was going to let the world know where Akron was. I didn't know how. I just knew in my heart I was going to do it.

Was I a dreamer?

Of course I was.

But if you wish hard enough, try hard enough, find the right group of guys to dream along with you, then maybe, because there is always a maybe with dreams, they can come true.

2.

Saviors

I.

I was born in December 1984 in a house on Hickory Street that was mostly maintained by my mom's mother. She was a wonderful woman who helped us out a lot. But when I was three, my grandmother died early Christmas morning of a massive heart attack at the age of forty-two. Typical of my mom, she did not tell me until I had opened up all my presents, including one of those little plastic basketball hoops (just for the record, I did slam it down).

The house was a large and sweeping Victorian with a front porch and foyer and grand living room and television room and kitchen and pantry downstairs and four bedrooms upstairs. It had been in my mother's family for generations, and at one time the grounds included horses, a goat named Katrina, blackberry trees, pear trees, and a grapevine. When my grandmother died, the house on Hickory Street became harder and harder to keep up. My mom was working any-where and everywhere to somehow make ends meet, including a stint at a toy store called Children's Palace. The house needed work, the plumbing and the electrical were failing: work on an old house takes money, and we didn't have money. Eventually, the city came in, served several eviction notices, and ultimately condemned it and bulldozed it to the ground.

Then the moves started. I guess I could have complained: being uprooted as a very young child is no way to live. Between the ages of five and eight, I moved twelve times. But complaining would do no good. It would only have put more pressure on my mom, who already felt guilty enough. I have never been much of a complainer anyway. So when the time came, I just grabbed my little backpack, which held all the possessions I needed, and said to myself what I always said to myself: It's time to roll.

Was there a certain tragedy attached to it? Of course there was a certain tragedy attached to it. Was there a danger attached to it? Of course there was a danger attached to it. Not just the police sirens and the gunfire in the various places we lived but the real danger that, like so many African American boys, I would just get lost in the very hardness of life. In fourth grade I missed close to a hundred days of school because it was across town, and we often didn't have the trans-portation to get there. That kind of life builds up a lack of trust, a feeling that what you care about and the friends you have made will disappear because you know, you just know, that you're going to be on the move, getting that little backpack ready because it's time to roll again.

The hardest thing for me was going to new schools and meeting new friends and finally getting comfortable with them and then having to leave and go to another school and getting comfortable again and then leaving again. Over and over, the cycle repeated itself.

At the same time it made me realize that wherever we were going, I would have to assume responsibility for myself. Like it or not, that's how my mom treated me. Sometimes I went to bed not knowing if I was going to see her the next morning. I would sometimes go a few nights without seeing her at all. I became afraid that one day I would wake up, and she would be gone forever.

It's all I really cared about when I was growing up, waking up and knowing that my mom was still alive and still by my side. I already didn't have a father, and I didn't want to be without both parents. All I could do was hope and pray that she was safe, because I knew she was trying to do the best for me that she could. And she always came back to me. She put food on the table for Thanksgiving like everyone else, and everything that I wrote down on the Christmas list always found its way under the tree. I don't know how she did it, and I never asked her how she did it. So as scary as it was at times, as tough as it was at times, it only made me love her more. Whatever my mom could do or could not do, I also knew that nobody was more important in her life than I was. You have no idea how much that means when you grow up without so many of the basic things you should have. You have no idea of the security it gives you, how it makes you think, Man, I can get through this. I can survive.

They were still tough times. When I was nine, my mom sat me down and told me that I would be living with a family called the Walkers until she could move her own life into a better situation. I know she hated to do it. But she felt backed into a place of no return and knew this would be the best for her and for me. It was unimaginable at first. I had never met my father, and the idea of losing my mother, even if it was temporary, frightened me. She promised she would visit me as much as she could. She promised that we would be reunited once she found a life that would give both of us stability.

At the time I played on a peewee football team called the East Dragons. The coaches there knew my situation, in particular that I was missing school. Some of them offered to take me in. But they were single men, trying to make sense of their own lives. There was some discussion that I might move in with relatives in Youngstown, but Frankie and Pam Walker came forward and suggested to my mom that I could stay with them, and she agreed. I had spent part of spring break with the Walkers, but when school resumed, I did not resume with it. The Walkers were also concerned that I was being passed from place to place, a nomad at the age of nine.

Pam Walker really didn't know me very well, nor did she know my mother well. She had concerns that because I was a good athlete beginning to get notice in Akron, I might overshadow her own son, Frankie Jr., who was about a year and a half younger than I was and a fine athlete in his own right. She worried that her son would feel like a backup. Frankie Walker knew me a little bit better because he had coached me on the East Dragons. It looked to him like there was little joy in my life, as if I was older than my actual age and had already seen too much and been through too much, as if I was trying to play the role of being a kid but really wasn't one. He saw someone who needed help, and once he discussed it with his family, the Walkers were willing to take me in.

I went to live with them for my fifth-grade year, under an arrangement where I spent the week with the Walkers and weekends with my mother. I was pretty sure that Frankie and Pam would accept me—they had agreed to take me in, after all—but I didn't know how their three children would feel about having a new addition to the family. So I was quiet at first. Chanelle, the oldest, didn't want anything to do with Frankie Jr. and me. If she had her druthers, we would have moved someplace else. We just got on her nerves. But Tanesha, the youngest sister, got along wonderfully with me and Frankie Jr., and to this day calls me her brother. Frankie Jr. and I also got along well together; we shared a room in a three-bedroom colonial on Hillwood Drive.

I now believe it was karma that placed me there. It was the year before, in fourth grade, that I had missed so many days of school. My grades had suffered. My life had suffered. I was never one to just hang out. I didn't like looking for trouble, because I didn't like trouble. But I was on the edge of falling into an abyss from which I could never escape.

The Walkers were disciplined, and they plunged me right into that discipline. Pam Walker woke all of us kids up at 6:45 a.m., assuming we had taken a bath the night before. If not, she woke us up at six. She made sure we washed behind the ears. We had chores to do, which is something I never had to contend with before. It could be doing the dishes in the kitchen and sweeping the floor and washing countertops and taking out the trash. It could be cleaning up our bedrooms and moving all of our junk out of the living room before Frankie Walker, or Big Frankie as he was known, came home.

The Walkers weren't instilling discipline in us for discipline's sake. They were teaching us how to behave, not just in their home but in the world. They were teaching us how to be responsible and take pride in that responsibility. The proof of it was in my attendance at school in fifth grade at Portage Path Elementary: I didn't miss a single day.

The Walkers laid a foundation for me, a foundation I really had never experienced before. I got the stability I craved. They showed me that living in a house in a family-style environment was the rule, the way most people lived their lives, not the exception. I adapted to it easily, maybe because, having already moved around so much in my life, I was good at dealing with new situations. I loved being there. I loved being part of the flow that is a family. I loved being with other kids. I began to show a sense of humor, and I didn't even mind when Frankie Jr. and I didn't go to bed on time and Big Frankie said we better do it before there was trouble; he was, after all, called Big Frankie for a reason. I saw how life was meant to be lived, as part of something essential and valuable and permanent. I appreciated Pam Walker's focus on education, because it turned out that I liked school once I regularly started going. I appreciated her telling me that keeping my grades up, combined with my athletic ability, could get me in to any college I desired (although it turned out a little differently).

The Walkers became family to me. Living with them changed my life. I felt wanted, and I felt the blessing of security. But my mom was still my mom. In sixth grade the roles reversed, and I stayed with her during the week and with the Walkers on the weekends. Then she lost the apartment she was living in, and I stayed with the Walkers again for a short time. There was discussion that I might move to Rochester, New York, but I had assimilated into the Walker family so much that Pam felt it would be like taking one of her children away if I moved to a different city. She had a friend who was a manager at the

Springhill apartments; that's when my mom and I moved into a two-bedroom unit under a rental-assistance program. The building had little terraces in front of each apartment. Otherwise it was spare and unadorned, almost Soviet-style, and incongruous with its surroundings as it stood on that little hill. Behind it was a taller high-rise that glowered like a darkened storm cloud, and most in Akron considered Springhill a shabby and undesirable place to live. But I had my own room. I had my mom with me again, and we would stay there until I finished high school. All of it felt good. All of it felt right. But without that time spent at the Walkers, I don't honestly know what would have become of me.

II.

I first started playing basketball when I was about nine with a team called the Hornets at the Summit Lake Community Center on Crosier Street in Southwest Akron. Frankie Walker was one of the coaches, and based upon my performance with the East Dragons in football, he asked me to play, so I did. Football was my first love. I played tailback and liked to think I was Deon Sanders or Eric Metcalf. I even wore the same number they did, 21. Scoring a touchdown was the ultimate. Even as a kid you could do that, whereas the ultimate in basketball was a dunk, and I was nowhere near tall enough to do that yet.

Even so, I took to the game of basketball instantly. I liked the adventure of putting the ball in the rim. I liked the team concept of basketball. I liked the pace of it, running up and down the court for four or five possessions without a time-out. Since defense is basically an abstract concept when you're a kid, I liked gambling for steals so you could score on a breakaway layup.

I played on the Hornets for a year. It was also around that time I placed my basketball life in the hands of a man, maybe the most special man I have ever met, with a heart that was beautiful and bountiful. His name was Dru Joyce II, and that's where the first seeds of the dream all sprout from.

As you can probably tell by now, I look for karma. I believe that things happen for a reason or don't happen for a reason. I believe it was karma that connected me to Coach Dru, which is what we always called him.

Coach Dru graduated from Ohio University in 1978. He got a job at Hunt-Wesson Foods in Pittsburgh in sales, and after a few years was promoted to the position of senior sales rep, with a territory that included Cleveland and the eastern suburbs. By all rights, Coach Dru and his family, which now included two daughters, should have settled in the Cleveland area. Had he lived there, I never would have met him; without meeting him, who could predict what would have happened to me. A district manager at Hunt-Wesson suggested he settle in Akron, which was a little cheaper than Cleveland, and Coach Dru took his advice. He moved there with his family in March 1984, but it was only supposed to be temporary. After a year or so, he figured he would move to Cleveland. But there was something about Akron he liked—the size of it, the feel of it, even the smell of it, because a few companies were still making rubber products back then, and every afternoon you could catch the sharp aroma. So he stayed, living in an apartment first before moving to a house on Greenwood Avenue in

West Akron. Because he stayed, my life changed, just as it had with the Walkers.

There was something else he wanted beyond being a good provider. He wanted to coach kids, and he was desperate to have a son. After his first two children were girls, I think he was getting a little bit worried, even though he loved those daughters to death. He was just one of those fathers who needed a son. When it finally happened in January 1985, he had a little trouble actually believing it. He and his wife, Carolyn, were in the delivery room in the hospital together when that son was born. Coach Dru was so overcome that he walked away from Carolyn just to stare at him, make sure he was real, had the essential equipment. Finally, his wife had to call him back to make sure he remembered that she was real too and had just gone through the hell of giving birth.

They named their son Dru Joyce III. I wasn't there at the birth, of course, but as I got to know Little Dru, because that's what everybody called him, I am pretty sure he came out kicking and screaming.

Coach Dru didn't waste any time getting Little Dru involved in sports. Football had been Coach Dru's first love, so he slated Little Dru as a wide receiver and had him running pass patterns when he was three. Little Dru didn't like football, and knowing Little Dru as I do now, I am also pretty sure that he had no problem letting his father know it. So Coach Dru switched his son to tennis, and Little Dru was good. On Saturday mornings his dad played several hours of pickup basketball at the Elizabeth Park Community Center with some men from his church. Little Dru tagged along, and even though he was only four or five, he began picking up the nuances of the game just by watching. For most of the time we played together, he was a puny little pipsqueak (sorry, Little Dru, but you know it's the truth). He had big ears that stuck out like gigantic stereo speakers, so he was always a little bit goofy looking (sorry, Little Dru, but you know it's the truth). He was so quiet, sometimes I thought he really wanted to be one of those monks who take a vow of silence.

He also had that little man complex. It motivated him to be great because there were so many who said he was too small to ever be great in basketball, ever be much of anything, just a little kid coming along for the ride. People sometimes laughed at him and called him "pixie" and "smurf," which only motivated him more. It also made him emotionally trigger-happy, the kind of kid who would take on anybody, no matter what the size, if he thought he had just been insulted.

I like poking fun, and I remember crossing the line with Little Dru at a church retreat we both went to one summer. We got into an argument over a pillow, of all things. He was angry, like anybody who has the name "Little" in front of his name is always going to be angry, always has to prove that little in size does not mean little in pride and work ethic and courage. He thought I had stolen his pillow, so he pushed me and I pushed him back. I never thought he would hit me because I was so much taller and stronger, but then he did anyway. I didn't want to hurt him by retaliating, so I just threw him across the room. Even Little Dru knew there were moments in life when the only option was surrender: "I just grabbed my pillow and went to bed."

He was also inexhaustible. In sixth grade, when I was at the Joyces much of the time, I played one-on-one with Little Dru. Eventually I had to quit, because he refused to give up even though I was always beating him: "I'm not going to stop—you got to keep playing." It was the same with his father. They played in the driveway, where there was a basketball hoop attached to the garage. Coach Dru, trying to toughen his son up a little bit, always won. But Little Dru wouldn't have it. He sometimes made his father stay out there until midnight, until Coach Dru just gave him a victory so he could go to bed.

With his combination of combativeness and perfectionism, we eventually started to think of him as "the General." You know how it is with generals. You mess at your own risk. He didn't mince words. He didn't know how to mince words. Whether it was rec-league basketball or traveling team basketball or whatever kind of basketball, there was always one constant—if you screwed up on the court, Little Dru was going to march up to you and let you know. Like I said, the General. And the first piece of the dream, along with his father.

3.

East Liverpool

I.

It was a moment of impulse, but one day Coach Dru took his son to see his roots. He thought it was important for Little Dru, who then was thirteen or fourteen, to appreciate the difference in how he had been raised. The Joyce family at that point was solidly middle-class, living in the house on Greenwood with three bedrooms and a fully finished attic and a recreation room downstairs. His father, along with his mother, who worked part-time for a nonprofit organization that encouraged middle-schoolers to stay away from sex and drugs and other potentially dangerous vices, had achieved the American dream. But there was a time when that dream had seemed impossible for Coach Dru, a faraway point that would never be reached.

East Liverpool, Ohio, was a town of about 20,000 in that little pocket where Ohio and West Virginia and Pennsylvania all merge together, classic rust belt. Coach Dru's dad was a janitor there, working for the First National Bank and a local jewelry store. His mom was a day worker, a fancy way of saying that she cleaned rich people's homes. To make extra money, his parents sometimes served dinner at the local country club. His house was up on a hillside on a dirt road. It was brown with a cracked concrete slab out front that served as a porch. When it rained, they put buckets all over the upstairs to catch the leaks, and sometimes parts of the ceiling fell in. Until he was in eighth grade, his family had one of those old coal furnaces. The coal company came and dumped the coal on the hillside. The Joyce family built a little barrier with wooden stakes so the coal wouldn't just roll downhill. Coach Dru came with a little box and carried the coal into the dirt floor of the cellar over and over, until the job was finished. The only organized sport he played was football, but since the family didn't have a car until seventh grade, he walked with his cousin to practice two miles up and down the hills that dotted the region, and then back again after practice.

Coach Dru's mom scrimped and saved and made sure that he got whatever he needed, or at least as much as she could possibly afford. Until he was six, Coach Dru shared a bedroom with his grandmother. She died, and the room still had the same battered furniture. It stayed that way until Coach Dru came home one summer day at the age of nine to a new bedroom set. Without telling him, his mom had quietly purchased it on layaway. It had taken her at least a year, but that's the type of woman she was, determined to do the best for her son. Coach Dru never thought of himself as poor, in large part because of the way his mom and dad fought to provide for him, and it was only in filling out financial aid applications for college that he realized just how low the family's income was, about $8,000 a year in the early 1970s.

After graduation from East Liverpool High School, Coach Dru went to Ashland College in Ohio. He had been a pretty good receiver in high school, and he went there intending to continue football. But football and Coach Dru didn't mix well at Ashland. He didn't have the driving force he felt he needed, and Ashland began to feel small to him, too small, like being back in high school. That summer he got a job at Crucible Steel, across the Ohio River in Midland, Pennsylvania. It was painless lifting, in an office that was away from the soot and the furnaces and all the other hell that steel mills routinely churn out. He prepared samples of steel for chemical analysis by taking little shavings. He was often done early, and when he was through, he went and sat on a loading dock and watched community softball games. The money was good, and since Coach Dru didn't have a lot of it—still with only a couple of pairs of blue jeans to his name—the temptation to stay and forget about college was enormous. His mother told him to not even think about it. So he transferred to Ohio University, and while he partied harder than he should have, he found his calling in business. His mother must have had a sixth sense anyway, because two years after Coach Dru worked at Crucible Steel, the mill closed up. All his friends who had money in their pockets and cars and thought they were going to live the good life were now out of work.

That was the kind of life he led until he became the first member of his family to graduate from college, a life that was hard but lived without complaint because that's just how life was. I think I somehow knew that about Coach Dru the first time I met him when I was about nine. Something just told me. We just had that instant affinity for one another. I understood him, and he understood me. I trusted him, which is not something I did easily back in those days.

II.

Since Coach Dru lived in Akron, he knew where to find raw talent, one of the advantages of a place small enough so that word of athletic potential traveled fast. He knew about the Ed Davis Community Center near the Akron Zoo and the Summit Lake Community Center. Even in his own church, between the prayers and the hymnals and the sermon, he would scan the pews, looking for a kid who had some size on him and might be a defensive force.

That's how I first came into his life, through the Summit Lake rec center. He saw me play basketball, and he must have observed something that enticed him; I wasn't with the Walkers yet, but he found out where we lived, over in the projects in Elizabeth Park, and talked to my mom, Gloria, about joining an Amateur Athletic Union travel team called the Shooting Stars. The AAU, as it is known, is a national nonprofit entity that organizes leagues and tournaments on the amateur level in virtually every sport imaginable.

Coach Dru didn't know the backstory of my life. But I'm pretty sure he knew that my life had been a crazy quilt of moves there and moves here growing up until we finally landed in the forlorn red brick of Elizabeth Park. Up until then, it had been constant on-the-go, and so many different schools that I tried to lose count. Who ever wants to keep track of something like that? All it does is cause you pain and memories you would rather forget.

Coach Dru's circumstances were slightly different from mine. He did have two parents. But he knew the meaning of what it was like to be poor. Just as he also knew that sports, under the right conditions, could save a child's life. He also picked up right away that for all I had been through, I wasn't hardened or bitter. He liked the fact that I was friendly and curious about the world. While I downplayed it at the time, he knew in his heart that as an only child, I was desperate to be around other kids. I also liked the idea of joining the Shooting Stars because I heard they traveled to places as exotic as Cleveland, where I had never been before even though it was about half an hour away.

So after my mom's initial skepticism (she even insisted on going to the first practice to make sure Coach Dru was legitimate), she let me join the team.

Coach Dru was still on the lookout. You need at least five players to make up a basketball team, and the next piece of the dream came from church. The Joyce family went to the same church as the Cotton family, called the House of the Lord. Coach Dru and Lee Cotton had been Sunday school teachers together. Coach Dru knew that Lee Cotton had been a great high school basketball player in Akron; when he saw his son Sian in church one Sunday, there was something he liked about him—his size. He was aware Sian was a good baseball player, which doesn't automatically translate into skill in basketball, but he also realized he could take up a lot of essential space on the court. Sian had a personality to match his size, funny on the outside but fearless and a little bit of a renegade on the inside, a natural-born intimidator. If you didn't want to mess with Little Dru when he told you something, because he wouldn't ever let it go, you also didn't want to mess with Sian. So he became the third piece of the dream as a player.

Sian came from a sturdy family. They lived over in Goodyear Heights, a tidy section of two-story homes built for workers from the various Goodyear plants that had once dotted the city. His dad, Lee, had been a longtime courier for FedEx. His mom, Debra, did occasional temporary work, but largely stayed home to take care of Sian and his older brother, L.C.

Basketball was simply alien to Sian. He couldn't make a layup to save his life, and Little Dru's exasperation would become palpable: "I'm passing you the ball, and you can't score. That's a problem." So was the fact that Sian traveled constantly. In baseball he could go out without any practice and throw no-hitters. In basketball he was growing so quickly that he was still trying to catch up to his body. I would never say this about Sian, because I love him too much, but he has a pretty good assessment of how he played that first year we were all together:

"I was kind of a bum."

Little Dru knew more about the game than anyone at the time, including his dad. Even when he was nine and ten, you could see those fundamentals taking hold. I, on the other hand, had no use for fundamentals despite what Frankie Walker had taught me, not back then. I could tell that it drove Little Dru right to the edge. The first time he saw me play, it was like I was trying to make a highlight reel, behind-the-back passes and all other sorts of nonsense and the ball flying in every which direction all over the court. I could feel Little Dru's anger boiling up even then.

So Coach Dru, who had become the coach because of his volunteer work with the Shooting Stars the year before, had a long journey ahead. He also believed he could take the raw talent that was there and maybe mold it into something. Because his only experience in basketball had been as a pickup player, he willed himself to become a coach. He ultimately bought every book and tape on basketball he could find, his favorite being *The John Wooden Pyramid of Success*. Little Dru went to camps and clinics, and Coach Dru usually accompanied him, then bent the ear of any coach he could seek out to further learn the game.

Little Dru in turn had that streak of perfectionism—he insisted on doing the drills until he had them exactly right—so Coach Dru would work with him at home. As for me, I was a good natural athlete. Sian was, well, Sian, strong and able to play defense, although approval from Little Dru was still not forthcoming: "We had to use him for something." Little Dru's theory was pretty simple—if your fingertips touched the basketball, you should catch the basketball. So even if the pass was a little bit wild, if your fingertips touched it, it was on you as far as Little Dru was concerned. Then he would yell at you for not catching it, so Sian got yelled at quite a bit. But Sian was almost six-one, so big that he could only play one year of peewee football because of weight limitations, and he could easily take what Little Dru spewed out.

We started out in 1996 in a red-brick building on Maple Street that housed the Salvation Army. The walls were a dingy white, with the Salvation Army logo painted in the middle. The gym was tiny, about twenty feet less in length than a regulation court. The floor was made of linoleum; playing on it was like dribbling in your kitchen. But that was the best we could find. We were in fifth grade, playing with a lot of sixth-graders, then the sixth-graders left to form their own team, and we were basically the only ones left. A few more boys were added so we would have enough players, and we played well. In fact, the Shooting Stars qualified for the national AAU tournament in Cocoa Beach, Florida, that summer for kids eleven and under.

At first Coach Dru didn't want to go. Getting to Florida was expensive, and there was no way we could fly there. But one of the dads, Kirk Lindeman, just couldn't let go of the opportunity that lay before us. One day, he turned to Coach Dru and said, "Let's do this. They may never qualify for a national championship again in their life."

Coach Dru realized that Lindeman was right, and they found a way to do it.

We had only seven players on the team when we piled into Coach Dru's minivan and headed off to Florida with Little Dru's mom and two sisters and little brother in another car with food so we would have something to eat on the way down. We were kids from Akron, the Rubber Capital of the World that wasn't even that anymore, and for us, going to Cleveland was a long trip. Now we were heading to Florida for the AAU tournament. It was there in Cocoa Beach that I saw the ocean for the first time with all that water rushing in, inching into it toe by toe before I started joyously splashing around with some of the other players like the kids we still were.

We didn't know what to expect in terms of the tournament. We found sixty-odd other teams there, some of them from the big basketball meccas of Houston and Chicago and Southern California, decked

out in their fancy shoes and jackets and rip-away warm-ups and match-
ing bags. "We didn't care who we were going to play next," Little Dru
remembered. "It was just like, 'Look at their uniforms.'" The opening
ceremonies were at the Kennedy Space Center, like something out of
the Olympics, and Coach Dru also couldn't help but wonder what we
had just gotten ourselves into. He started talking with a fellow coach
in front of him as they lined up at the ceremony. The coach was going
on and on about how they were the number-one seed in the tournament. He mentioned a player on the team named J. R. Giddens, who
later went on to be drafted by the Boston Celtics with the thirtieth pick
out of the University of New Mexico. He talked about how they had
played about sixty-five games together. The newly constituted Shooting Stars had played about seven games together, and all Coach Dru
could say to himself was, This doesn't look good. This doesn't look
good at all.

But basketball is about finding the right parts and putting them
together. There was the cohesiveness of Little Dru and Sian and
me, since we had played together earlier in the summer. We added
a player named Grant Urbanski, who was a great shooter and handled the ball well. We added Jim Lindeman's son Pat, who wasn't
very athletic and was a little bit slow, but could also shoot if he got
his feet set. We added Jarryd Tribble, who was willing to do the
scut work—setting up screens, rebounding, going for loose balls. We
added Vahn Knight, a superb all-around athlete who ran the ball
well and played defense well and shot well and went on to play at
Ashland University in Ohio.

Little Dru had those great fundamentals and a shot that seemed
to be on its way to becoming legendary. I was fast and loved offense

(defense I could do without). From the very beginning, Little Dru and I had this uncanny ability to understand each other on the court. Sian did hold the middle defensively, and he also improved considerably during the tournament as he gained confidence. The other players fulfilled their roles.

Somehow, we finished an astounding ninth out of the sixty-four teams there, even though we had barely played together. The three of us—Little Dru and Sian and I—were starting to develop a chemistry even then. And not just when we played basketball. We were beginning to gravitate toward each other off the court, much of it the result of that interminable 1,027-mile ride from Akron to Cocoa Beach. Because it doesn't matter who you are—after close to twenty hours in a minivan, you are going to know everything about your car mates, whether you like it or not. Silence is not permitted.

After the tournament, Coach Dru said something I will never forget. The championship game had ended, and they were giving out the trophies, and there was ours for ninth place, along with an equipment bag with the AAU insignia on it. Our hopes going down there had not been very high, so we were excited and exploding with confidence. We were packing up our gear to return to Akron, preparing for the ride from hell home, when Coach Dru just looked at his son and Sian and me. He appreciated the hardness with which we played, and more important, the passion. He said at that moment, "I don't know what it is, but you guys are going to do something special."

Even though we were still young, we somehow knew it too. The thought lay beneath the surface at that point. We couldn't really articulate it. When we came back to Akron, there was no real buzz, just a bunch of kids who had done well in an AAU tournament. Yet the seeds were already forming, something we wanted to fulfill before we were through. The dream began to swirl around in our young minds that the following summer we could do better than ninth place, maybe even achieve the miracle of winning a major national championship one day.

If we got more pieces.

4.

Willie McGee

I.

Willie McGee was all resilience. Probably the reason for that was his youth on the west side of Chicago, which, as he once put it, "will swallow you whole, good family or not." He came from a good family, his grandmother Lena the backbone of it, tough and strong. She commanded respect in a neighborhood that was rife with drugs and gangs. Willie lived with her as a young boy, in a two-family duplex at the corner of Kedzie and Arthington near Chicago Stadium, where the Bulls used to play. Lena was a savvy entrepreneur, running a diner in the front of the house. She sold soul food and deli sandwiches and rib dinners. She even had a snowball stand at one point. But she was getting up in years, and there was just so much she could do with Willie. His mother and father were going through difficult times, struggling with drug addictions, taking everything from crack to snorting heroin, and Willie started being looked after by his sister Makeba, who was thirteen years older.

Willie felt like he owed his life to Makeba because of how she basically mothered him when he was young. Once she took him to the doctor to get a shot, and he was so resistant that he kicked the nurse. She always kept him fed, although it might be sausage and rice and toast for a week because money was so tight. Makeba's life wasn't easy. She had two small children of her own. She was also looking after Willie's younger brother, Patrick, as their mother, Dale, appeared and then disappeared because of her addiction to crack. Whenever she left, Willie would grab her leg and plead, "Mama, stay here with me, don't go." But Dale, as she later said, "just had to," the lure of the streets and the parties too hard to overcome.

The responsibility placed on Makeba was monumental, and when Makeba had to run an errand, it was Willie, as the oldest at six or seven, who changed his niece and nephew and youngest brother's diapers. He warmed up their bottles and he fed them and made sure they burped and put them to sleep. There was usually an uncle or cousin living upstairs, so if Willie got into trouble and accidentally started a fire or something, there was someone to turn to. He took his responsibilities with seriousness and purpose despite being so young. But he was missing school, close to forty days at Bethune Elementary one year. Looking back on it, Willie himself could predict what would have eventually happened, that the lure of easy drug money on the corner might land him in jail.

When he was seven, he spent the summer in Akron with his brother Illya, a former high school basketball star at Providence St. Mel School in Chicago who had been recruited by the University of Akron. The drugs and the gangs in the neighborhood were only getting worse, and when the day came for him to leave for Akron in 1987, his grandmother Lena took Illya aside and said, "Don't come back." She kissed him and she cried and said he should visit his family, and then she told him once more, "This is not where you need to be."

Illya, who was fourteen years older than Willie, had always wanted a baby brother. He got that wish on January 1, 1984, when Willie was born. It became clear as time went on that Willie idolized his brother, wanted to follow in his exact footsteps, excelling in basketball in high school and then getting a college scholarship. Illya returned that love. Willie came to his basketball games at Providence St. Mel, and Illya brought him into the locker room afterward and took Willie to practices. Both Illya and Makeba sheltered him from the streets. One Christmas, Willie's grandmother had given his parents money to buy Christmas presents for her grandson. They spent almost all of it on drugs, and there were no gifts under the tree. Willie's mother had about twenty dollars left, and Illya and Makeba scratched up some more. Illya went to stores in Chicago that sold items for a dollar or two and bought up all the gifts he could find. When Willie awoke Christmas morning, there were dozens of presents under the tree. It meant that Illya and Makeba went without gifts of their own, but the look on Willie's face was enough Christmas for them.

The bond between Willie and Illya was unbreakable, so much so that Illya became terribly homesick when he went to the University of Akron. He wanted to return home, in large part because of Willie. He thought about him all the time, and he worried about the ups and downs of drugs, which he believed were affecting the family.

When the opportunity arose for Willie to spend the summer with Illya and his girlfriend, Vikki, in Akron, the bond reignited immediately. Illya and Vikki spoiled Willie, giving him his own bedroom and buying him bushels of clothes. They took him to his first movie, his first real restaurant, his first buffet, his first mall, his first amusement park, Geauga Lake Amusement Park near Cleveland, where Willie rode everything from the roller coaster to the bumper cars like the seven-year-old child he was but never had been.

The end of that summer was maybe the hardest time Illya ever experienced. He knew he had to take Willie back to Chicago, but it devastated him. He just counted off the days, and when the time came, they got into the car and made the six-hour trip on the Ohio Turnpike and then the Indiana Toll Road. They talked some, but the ride over the eternal flatness was long and only made longer as Illya tried to prepare himself for what he had to say. They stayed in Chicago three days, with Willie clinging to Illya almost the whole time. The moment came, and as much as Illya had tried to prepare for it, he realized there was no way he could ever prepare for something like this.

He went into the back room of the house with Willie and Makeba, and she said, "You know, Illya has to go back."

"Can I go?" asked Willie.

"No," said Illya. It was his senior year at college, and he had to finish.

Willie started to deteriorate in front of Illya's eyes.

"Willie, it will be all right. I'll be back."

"No, no, no. I want to go."

Willie started to cry. So did Illya. He hugged him and gave him a kiss and told him that he loved him and was going to send him something wonderful for Christmas. He couldn't look back. He just had to keep going because there was no other place to go, because he felt that everything was crashing in around him. He felt that he had betrayed his younger brother, that the one person he looked up to and had faith in had just torn down his mountain. He worried that Willie was going to lose faith and trust in him.

Vikki was with him on the ride back to Akron. Illya could barely talk, he was still so overcome. It was on the Indiana Toll Road that Vikki just blurted it out:

"You know what we have to do, don't you?"

"No."

"You know we've got to bring him back. He just did so much better with us. He's going to have a better opportunity."

Illya had actually been thinking the same thing. But he wasn't married to Vikki yet—they married in 1995—and he was concerned that it was too much to ask of her.

"Are you ready for something like that?"

"Yeah, I am."

"Wow," was all Illya could say in return.

For the next several weeks he made sure that Vikki truly understood the responsibility of having a child live permanently with them. Afterward he called his family and got the blessings of Makeba and their mother. Illya told Willie next, and Willie started screaming and yelling through the house.

"Illya said I'm moving in with him! Illya said I'm moving in with him!"

The agreement was that Illya and Vikki wouldn't take Willie until the middle of the summer, so he could finish school. But every day Willie would come home and say to Makeba, "When is school over with? When is school over with?"

The middle of the summer finally came, and Makeba packed his clothing into a trash bag because they couldn't afford a suitcase. She made sure there were six or seven changes of clothes that were clean and washed and ready to go. With equal amounts of tears and guilt she took him to live with his brother, who was about to finish up at the University of Akron. It was terribly painful for her. She cried when she brought his meager possessions down to the car, a silver Honda Accord, and put them in the trunk and told him to be good and to listen. Willie drove off with Illya and Vikki and just kept looking back and looking back, feeling an emptiness that he had never felt before. He could see Makeba in the middle of the street, still crying. He could see the big berry tree in front of the house that messed up your clothes every summer when the berries dropped. As he kept looking, the finality of what was happening hit him: I'm leaving, and I'm leaving my sister. It was so terribly hard for Makeba. Willie didn't simply feel like a brother but one of her own children. But she knew he needed a male role model, someone strong and steady, someone who could not be found in the drug-strewn streets of west side Chicago.

The responsibility placed on Illya and Vikki was enormous, taking care of an eight-year-old. Illya was scared, and all sorts of thoughts raced through his mind: Am I going to be able to do it? Am I going to be the man I really think I am, or am I going to fail? As he rode back to Akron that day, he also said to himself, Lord, just stay with me and show me the way. Just show me the way.

That first night, Willie went into the bedroom where he had stayed the summer before and saw the Superman bedspread crisp and new. He saw the television. He was elated and excited. So were Illya and Vikki. They all sat up much of the night just talking, and when Willie finally went to bed, Illya must have peeked in on him ten times just to remind himself that he was truly there, thinking to himself that in the six-hour trip from Chicago to Akron, Willie McGee had literally traveled from darkness to light.

For as long as Willie could remember, he had always had a basketball in his hands. When he had been living in Chicago, he often played at a parking lot across the street from his house, where there were four sets of hoops. It was different in Akron. They lived near the university campus in a two-bedroom apartment on South Adams Street, across from Akron City Hospital. There weren't many kids around like there had been in Chicago, and Illya had just started working full time for the Ohio Community Corrections Association—basically a halfway house called Oriana—as a resident supervisor. Vikki was working there as well. Willie felt lonely at times, and he still had his Chicago tendencies: when he was riding in the car one day, someone mentioned that they needed to go to the drive-thru of a local store, and Willie thought she said drive-by and immediately ducked his head.

Illya and Vikki responded to the challenge. They clothed him. They fed him. They taught Willie morals. They taught him how to be responsible and respectful and take pride in himself. They took Willie to the malls at Chapel Hill and Rolling Acres, where they inevitably bought something for him, whether it was the newest in sneakers or the newest in trendy clothes. They took him out to eat at his favorite restaurant, Red Lobster, where Willie invariably ordered what Illya did, except for French fries instead of mashed potatoes. They took Willie to the library and to the movies and to plays.

Illya also took Willie to the downtown YMCA on Canal Square on Mondays and Wednesdays and Fridays and started teaching him the finer points of basketball, how to hold his hands, layups over and over and over, talking trash to him so he would toughen up and not be a baby on the court if someone tried to get between his ears. He pushed Willie around and smacked his hands, and Willie hated that, but it was all part of becoming a basketball player. Illya then got him involved with the Summit Lake Hornets, where he played with me and won a championship.

It was also Illya who consoled Willie and counseled him when it became clear that, because of what he had been through in Chicago, he needed special education help in reading and writing. Willie didn't want to be placed in any special education classes—it had a stigma attached that embarrassed him; he feared that other students would make fun of him. But Illya made it clear to Willie that he must have the help in order to catch up, a reality that set in when Illya realized that Willie could not read his middle name. Willie trusted his brother, and he became determined to get out of special ed as quickly as possible. He did just that, entering in the fourth grade and testing out in the middle of sixth grade. He continued to get good grades. Illya, in his role as surrogate father and mentor, didn't shower him with rewards when the report cards came around. He expected Willie to do well, and Illya's attitude rubbed off, because that's what Willie began to expect from himself.

There was something about Willie that just carried weight, the kind of kid you could always depend on, count on, a steady influence.

If somebody was about to do something silly or stupid, it was Willie who would say, "Hey, we're not getting into that." There was a maturity to him, a determination to overcome whatever had to be overcome. It also became clear that Willie was one of the best junior high basketball players in the city of Akron, a kid for whom sports could be so integral if he could find the right outlet.

So Willie became the next piece of the dream, along with me and Sian and Little Dru. He came in seventh grade. He played for an AAU team called the Akron Elite, and Coach Dru had his eye on Willie. When his team lost in the qualifying round for the national tournament, he was able under the rules to join another unit, and he hooked up with the Shooting Stars. Coach Dru liked the toughness with which he played, how he wasn't afraid of Sian like everyone else when he matched up with him. He liked Willie's relentless hustle. He also had size. He was about six-two at the time, and even Little Dru, who wasn't impressed by much, knew Willie was a player, a potentially great player, because he had competed against him. As Little Dru later put it, "He could handle the ball. He could defend. He could rebound. He could score." Some were predicting that he might grow as tall as six-seven, so Willie's potential seemed unlimited. There was no hint of the adversity he would later have to overcome.

II.

The year before, in 1997, without Willie, we made our bid to qualify for the twelve-and-under AAU national championships in Salt Lake

City. To even think about making the trip, we needed money, so we walked door-to-door to ask for donations, or stood on Akron street corners begging for money like the homeless you see with their signs of desperation. Thanks to a business colleague, Coach Dru also came up with something perfect for us to sell—duct tape.

We got a few hundred cases for free from a company, since the Shooting Stars were a nonprofit entity. We went door-to-door with thick rolls in hand, and we started to set aside some money in case we qualified. It all depended on the season we had, so Coach Dru added five more players to the nucleus of seven that had competed in Cocoa Beach. There was also radical improvement from Sian. Although he had gotten better during the tournament in Cocoa Beach, getting the ball to him, even for an easy layup, was still a hit-or-miss proposition. Sian's father, Lee, took his son's performance personally. He knew he had the tools to be a good player. After that first season, Lee took Sian to the YMCA every Saturday and relentlessly worked with him, refining his coordination, teaching him the game in general. The difference was remarkable. I was better, and so was Little Dru. Vahn Knight continued to be a key player, as was Grant Urbanski.

Always aware that his experience in basketball was limited, Coach Dru still became determined to run practices differently, not just roll the balls out. He enlisted the help of Lee Cotton and Jarryd Tribble's father, James, and practices actually became practices. Fundamentals were gone over again and again—shooting drills, passing drills, defensive drills. The coaches started teaching us the art of recognizing a zone defense and how to attack it. Before, we had been kind of run-and-gun, but now, since we were running into so many zone defenses, the coaches put in some offensive plays to combat them.

Typically, Coach Dru continued to get his hands on every book about basketball he could find. He also did research on the Web, finding strategies that were effective yet simple enough for us to understand.

We played about sixty games that summer. All of them were tournaments, and we won about 70 percent of them. Locally we had trouble; a team from Shaker Heights called the Shaker Heat beat us, as well as a team from Columbus. But we won the AAU qualifier to get to Salt Lake City. With the money that we had raised, we were able to fly. It was my first plane ride, and since it was my first plane ride, I might as well confess:

I cried like there was no tomorrow, scared out of my wits, my ears an impacted mess because of the altitude.

Salt Lake City was just as intimidating as Cocoa Beach had been the year before. When we registered, the first team we ran into, the Atlanta Celtics, had three kids who were six-five. Here we were with Sian at six-two, me at five-ten, and Little Dru at about four-eight. But Sian had gotten so much better that he might have been the best player on our team. The rest of us played well, defeating a team from Springfield, Missouri, that we had lost to the prior year. We were ultimately beaten by a team from Florida, finishing tenth overall.

We often hung out at Coach Dru's house when we weren't playing basketball, a tangle of bodies in the basement rec room with its off-white paneling, green indoor-outdoor carpeting, and drop-down ceiling. We played such video games as NBA Live, where Sian and I liked the Chicago Bulls and Little Dru liked the Phoenix Suns because of Kevin Johnson. Occasionally we played Madden football, as well as football on our knees on that indoor-outdoor carpeting. Sometimes Coach Dru would come down and couldn't quite figure who was there and who wasn't. But he trusted us, and at least he knew where we were, tossed about in sleeping bags or on the old couch. We tore that rec room apart, we were down there so much, because we couldn't get enough of each other. When we got tired of the rec room, we went outside, where the basketball hoop was attached to the garage. Then we put one of those Little Tikes hoops down the driveway at the other end to play the closest thing we could to full-court basketball.

III.

When Willie got dropped off for the first time at Coach Dru's house, Little Dru was doing homework and didn't say a word. I was there too, and all I managed was a halfhearted "What's up." Little Dru finally introduced himself as he put the basketballs in his dad's car. We rode to Cleveland for practice, because we were always riding all over the area to find someplace to practice. Coach Dru was berating Little Dru for something he had done at school, so there wasn't much opportunity for talking. Sian joined and was a little bit more forthcoming. We were still in that feeling-out process anyway, treating each other like a cat behaves when it paws about in a new room, those tentative steps of suspicion.

Until we got on the court. It was the music we needed, because basketball is a kind of music, jazzy at times and rap at times and balls-to-the-wall heavy metal at times. We were playing not at each other but with each other. Willie could see right away the love we had for the game, just as we saw it in him, and things quickly softened.

Soon after, he spent the night with me and Sian at my little apartment over in Springhill, and my mom cooked dinner. We started playing the usual video games together, and then things got really quiet, and we both said to Willie, "You pretty cool." For a kid who had been uprooted from his home, those few words were among the best he'd ever heard. It was a way of giving respect in the way that young kids give respect and also saying that we were all about the same thing: winning and taking care of business on and off the court. All for one and one for all.

The four of us—Little Dru, Sian, Willie, and I—began to be with each other whenever we could. We shared everything with each other, and it became a kind of unspoken rule—if you're eating something, everybody gets a piece, pizza, Starbursts, the thin sticks of Twizzlers, it didn't matter. All for one and one for all.

The Shooting Stars were good that season following Salt Lake City, very good. We played between sixty and seventy games that year; the Shaker Heat no longer beat us. We were defeating all the teams we played from Ohio, and traveling out of state to play in tournaments against teams from West Virginia and Indiana. We struggled against teams from Indiana, losing two tournaments. We also struggled against the Akron Elite. We managed to beat them in the AAU qualifier for thirteen-year-olds, which is when we went after Willie. He did everything that game, rebounded and shot well and dribbled.

We drove to Memphis in a passenger van for the national tournament. After finishing ninth in the AAU nationals in Cocoa Beach and tenth in Salt Lake City, we had high expectations, were ready to "make some noise," as Coach Dru later put it, perhaps win the national championship that we had been thinking about more and more.

Almost immediately we discovered a distraction—the pool at the motel. We were in it almost all the time in between games, which tired us out. Plus there were the girls. They were at the pool. We were at the pool, with just enough hair under our arms to discover the hormones of attraction. The flirting between the sexes was inevitable, and as Coach Dru later put it, "The quality time they were spending was at the pool, not the basketball court."

It didn't help that the first grouping we were placed in that year was loaded, and we finished third. That put us in the classic bracket, a gentle euphemism for the losers' bracket. We lost focus, played poorly, and ended up falling to the Missouri Skywalkers in the first game to get knocked out of the tournament. Even though it was July Fourth in Memphis, with a fireworks show and spectacular events that a bunch of kids from Akron had never seen and wanted to see, Coach Dru had had enough.

"We're packing up and going home," he told us. "This isn't what this is about. You all lost, there's no celebration here. I have given up so much of my time, and so have the rest of the parents, and if you guys aren't going to take this seriously, then hey, there's no point."

We didn't say anything. We just piled back into the passenger van and headed back to Akron. We were upset at missing out on all the sights and sounds that beckoned in Memphis. Even Coach Dru's wife, Carolyn, wasn't so crazy about just packing up and leaving. He was trying to teach us a lesson, perhaps the most important lesson you can learn, not only in basketball but in life: always perform with excellence. Losses happened, and Coach Dru understood that. It was our attitude that bothered him—lackadaisical, other preoccupations on our minds. He wanted us to understand that distractions had pulled us away from the goal we had set for ourselves, that major national championship. He wanted us to understand that every time you lose focus, you will suffer.

There were some positives. A solidarity was taking shape, team-mate protecting teammate, brother protecting brother. During the tournament we played a game, and afterward, when we lined up to shake hands, a player pushed Little Dru. Of course, Little Dru didn't budge an inch: he got right up into the player's face, nose to nose. Willie stepped in and pushed the other player, because he didn't like one of his teammates being treated like that. Sian's dad Lee took Willie aside and said, "That's not how we perform." Willie explained the situation, how he was watching out for a teammate, and Coach Dru, who had seen what had happened, confirmed the incident. Lee Cotton softened a little bit. He realized—as did we—that Willie, who was so quiet you couldn't exactly know what he thought or how he felt, was like the rest of us, loyal to a fault.

Even in the debacle of Memphis, something powerful was forming. Despite our age, the bond between us was built on much more than basketball. We were still kids. We still crossed the line, I most of all. I couldn't resist picking at the chip on Little Dru's shoulder or pointing out those funny ears of his. Or I'd make fun of Willie's silence, or Sian's wide body and the way he once cut his hair in the shape of a bowl. There were times we almost got into fights. Because that's what happens when you create a bond with someone that close. You get out of line, you talk too much, say too much, then you patch it up and work it out.

We also knew Coach Dru was right—we had squandered something precious in Memphis, that once-in-a-lifetime ability to be special. We wanted to win a national AAU championship, and we wanted to win it for Akron, put it on the map even if the mapmakers never would. We wanted to achieve our dream. We also realized that this might be our last opportunity, given the possibility we would all be going to different high schools.

When the AAU tournament for fourteen-year-olds and under came around the following summer in Orlando, we knew this probably was it. Either we'd achieve our dream then and there—or we never would.

IV.

The Shooting Stars played almost eighty games that eighth-grade year in 1999. We lost only one tournament, the first one of the season. When it was time for the AAU nationals, we were ready, determined in a way we had never been before. We played well, then lost to the Houston Hoops in pool play, with two team members who would later become first-round NBA draft picks straight out of high school, Ndudi Ebi and Kendrick Perkins. We still moved into the championship bracket by finishing second, which meant we were playing teams with high seeds. Unlike other opponents, we refused to let ourselves be distracted, even by the irresistibility of Orlando. We never went to Walt Disney World. We never went to Universal Studios or Epcot. We didn't go to the pool where we were staying, because Coach Dru had forbidden us to. We were focused this time: on basketball. We started beating teams we had never defeated before—two teams from Indiana as well as the Missouri Skywalkers, who had embarrassed us so badly the year before. Little Dru, who now was five feet, maybe, realized he had to add another element to his game. When he was younger, he had been able to take the ball to the basket. Because of his height everyone started blocking his shot. He and his dad started working on his jumper. By the time Little Dru was in eighth grade, he was averaging at least three 3-pointers a game. He was also handling the ball well and not turning it over.

Willie was rebounding with toughness and had a nice little jumper from ten to twelve feet. He could guard players out on the wing who were big and athletic and good ball handlers. He shut down the Skywalkers' best player, who had hurt us the year before, and he actually made a 3-pointer toward the end to cement the victory. We all cringed because we didn't know what Willie was doing shooting from out there, but he made it, so you couldn't complain. Sian took on players in the post who were physical and outmuscled them.

Something else was happening that I can't deny: I was getting better, a lot better. I had grown to about six-two. I could see the court in a way that I had never quite seen it before, more than a mess of pieces that sometimes fit and sometimes did not fit. I liked running the floor. I liked going to the hoop. I liked the competition of moving in for a rebound. Most of all, I loved to pass and dish off to teammates and neutralize the double teams and even triple teams that were becoming more common even then. Because to me that was one of the great challenges of the game, one of its greatest beauties—finding the open man, getting teammates to excel.

I had also learned to dunk in the eighth grade. I had first tried it a couple of months earlier at the middle school I went to, Riedinger, in a teachers-versus-students game. It was during the warm-up, and I just thought, What the heck. During the game I did it again on a break-away and not over some hapless teacher's head, where there would be serious academic hell to pay afterward. I wasn't stupid.

We played the Southern California All-Stars in the final game. They were sponsored by Nike with shoes and bags and warm-ups and three different sets of uniforms. They looked fresh in their red-and-white Nike gear. They looked like a championship team. Up until then, I had felt good about the way the Shooting Stars looked. Now we looked terrible.

The Southern California All-Stars had a center about six-five and a power forward roughly the same height. They had a player who was six-one and could jump out of the gym, and a little guard with light-ning speed. They had been the AAU national champions as fifth-, sixth-, and seventh-graders, so the idea of facing a bunch of kids from Akron must have seemed like instant slaughter to them. Ohio was a football state, not a basketball state. If you wanted basketball, then you better push one state over to Indiana, home of Rick Mount and Damon Bailey and Larry Bird from French Lick and a million other legends who could hit a 3 from anywhere. The Southern California All-Stars were arrogant. They had players like Trevante Nelson and Wesley Washington, who would go on to become major stars in high school. They had swagger and they talked trash, and they liked making fun of us as bumpkins from Hicksville U.S.A. who still had outhouses. "You're still in it?" was their attitude.

I have since been to Southern California many times. It is a cool and beautiful place, filled with riches and glamour and secret palaces hidden in the pockets of the Hollywood Hills. But right then and there, I hated Southern California. I can tell you something else that I learned about basketball at that moment—don't ever dismiss another team before you have played them. Because it only revved us up even more, energized us even more, put a chip on our shoulders just like the one Little Dru always carried around as perpetual anchor and burden. These were snot-nosed kids. They might have thought Akron was Hicksville, but they didn't know Akron, and they didn't know us. We knew even then the value of brotherhood on the court, that it is a team who wins against great competition, never a single individual, no matter how dominant.

Right before the game, Coach Dru called into the locker room the original seven who had played at Cocoa Beach three years earlier.

"Look, it's been my dream to win a national championship, just like it's been yours. But I want you to know that you've given me everything that I could ever want from this. So I just want you guys to play and play well and be relaxed and no pressure. You don't have to win."

WE ARE PLAYING at the Milk House at Disney's Wide World of Sports in Orlando. The court has an insignia of Mickey Mouse, and it seems almost appropriate, as the Southern California All-Stars take a 15-point lead early in the game and are treating us like cartoon characters. They are doing whatever they want. We take a shot and miss, and they are fast and laying it up at the other end. Then comes the turning point, when the Shooting Stars collectively say to themselves, No, we're better than this, and we're not going to quit. The game starts to reverse itself in the third quarter when we make a steal and convert it into a layup. I break an opponent down, get to the rim, and pour it in.

By the fourth quarter we start cutting into the lead even more, and the crowd fires up, and that only produces more adrenaline. All of a sudden the kids from Akron are making the kids from Southern California in their Nike red and white sweat for every point. Sian is a vacuum on defense, playing like the defensive tackle that he will ultimately become in high school but also getting his share of buckets at the opposite end. Willie is fearless, all blood and guts. Little Dru is the General. I am in the zone. It gets to where we are only down by 5, then 3, then 1.

We have a shot at the lead, with 12 seconds left, and to this day, despite all the wonderful things that have since come my way, despite being a member of the U.S. Olympic team in 2004 and the one in 2008 that won the gold medal and going to the NBA finals in 2007 with the Cleveland Cavaliers and leading them in the play-offs the last two years, I am still haunted by what I did.

I break by my defender and see an opening in the lane, a clear line to the basket. I go that route, but a player from the weak side comes up and blocks the shot when I should have gone for the dunk. We immediately foul, and their player misses the first but makes the second. Coach Dru calls a time-out. We get possession back down by 2, and now there are only 4 seconds left, and I know it is up to me, because either we are going to go down with me shooting or win with me shooting.

I am able to get off one dribble on the inbounds.

Three seconds . . .

Two seconds . . .

One second . . .

I cast off from downtown, beyond the 3-point line, a good thirty-five feet away but still a clear shot. From my vantage point everything goes into that sensory flow of slow motion. It is almost like I am dreaming as I watch the trajectory of the ball and everybody is looking at it and the whole crowd is dead silent. And the ball just hits the rim and goes in. Win the game. Win an AAU national championship. Put Akron on the map. Fulfill not just my goal but the goal of my brothers Little Dru and Sian and Willie.

Until it pops out.

THE SoCal All-Stars respected us after that. They were excited about winning—you could see it in their eyes—but they had no idea it was going to be as competitive as it was. Their coaches conveyed a clear message: I'm glad this is over. Coach Dru was convinced that if the Shooting Stars had had 2 more minutes left, we would have won. We had turned it around. We had momentum in our favor. True to our word, we had not given up when it looked so hopeless at the beginning.

But our dream, which had started out as a tiny kernel in fifth grade, which we had been nurturing for the past four years, was gone. We were off to high school, and Coach Dru thought this was the last time he would ever coach us again.

5

The Decision

I.

We just couldn't let it go.

As early as the middle of eighth grade, we had already begun to consider the idea of going to the same high school so we could still play basketball together. It was the only way we felt we always could keep our dream alive. As Little Dru put it, "Let's go do something big; let's go do something special." The loss to the Southern California All-Stars had only confirmed the decision, because as far as we were concerned, a 2-point loss might as well have been a 50-point loss. We did not take a single moment of solace in coming close, in returning to Akron with second-place trophies. Little Dru felt so distraught he didn't even want to pick his up. We wanted to do the city proud, and second place was exactly that, second place. We wanted another chance to reverse the order of finish. We all still felt unsatisfied, the lost chance that forever gnaws, that final-second shot kissing the rim and then kissing back out still playing in my mind. I had to right that, because no feeling in basketball is worse than ending on a shot missed. Even now, when I practice, I will not leave the floor until I have made that last shot. It's all part of karma—you finish the same way you want to begin.

At first, the decision of where to go seemed natural and easy. The school of choice for skilled black athletes was Buchtel, a public high school in West Akron. Named after John R. Buchtel, a leading Akron industrialist and philanthropist who had been savvy enough to be an initial backer of Dr. Benjamin Goodrich after he founded his rubber company. The sprawling school had been built of red brick in 1931. Its entrance jutted out like a big box of crackerjacks and had two stories of classrooms on either side. It also had a basketball coach named Harvey Sims, who was considered the Phil Jackson of Akron, hip and smart and sharp and innovative.

Most people assumed that we'd be going to Buchtel. They had been to the Division II state finals in 1997 under Harvey Sims. And Sims had also made Coach Dru an assistant basketball coach there during our eighth-grade year, knowing that he had more influence on us than any other adult in Akron, as an actual father to one of us and a father figure to the rest of us. Sims, to this day, is adamant that he hired Coach Dru because he was a good coach. As Coach Dru tells it, his hiring was all part of "the deal" of getting the four of us to Buchtel. He felt he knew why he was there, and he made no bones about it—to deliver us to Sims.

Buchtel made perfect sense to me. I knew the athletic reputation of the school; every black kid in Akron did. I was already having fantasies about how it would be: the four us marching in as Big Men on Campus who would lead Buchtel to a state and national championship, and best of all, the prettiest girls in the entire city. Coach Dru might have banned us from the motel pool ever since Memphis, but he couldn't ban us from talking to girls in the school hallways.

During "open gyms" at Buchtel in eighth grade, which were basically informal tryouts, Little Dru sensed that the coaching staff saw no immediate future in him—too short, too scrawny, too little of everything. Buchtel was stacked for the coming year, and there was no way Little Dru would make the varsity. He would have to start on the junior varsity team, methodically work his way up, and Little Dru simply didn't want to go that route. He wanted a chance to compete for the varsity, and he knew he wouldn't get it at Buchtel. The coaches there respected his cerebral style of play. They respected his fundamentals. To me at least, they made the mistake that most coaches make, whatever the level in basketball—they valued size over the incessant beating of a hungry heart. They didn't care that Little Dru would work on his game as long as he had to. They didn't care about that chip on his shoulder that had become his almost maniacal motivator. They didn't see the fearlessness behind the quiet exterior. They didn't see a kid who would not back down from anyone, no matter how outmatched.

The Shooting Stars had a major rivalry with a team from Huntington, West Virginia. They had a point guard who was bigger and stronger than Little Dru, but it didn't matter. The guard put a hard foul on Little Dru, and the ref didn't call it, and, Little Dru being Little Dru, we just knew what was going to happen next. When Huntington inbounded, Little Dru fouled the guard as hard as he could. His father pulled him aside and said, "Okay, we're done with that." They inbounded again. Little Dru fouled the guard as hard as he could again. They inbounded again. Little Dru fouled the guard as hard as he could again. His dad yanked him off the court and into the locker room. Coach Dru was so angry with his son that one of the assistant coaches had to pull him off. But Little Dru insisted that what he had done was right. "He fouled me hard, and he isn't getting away with that," he told his dad. Coach Dru knew, like we all did, that you could talk to Little Dru forever, making logical point after logical point, and he still wouldn't change.

Little Dru didn't think that anyone at Buchtel had slighted him. He had great respect for Coach Sims. It was just a feeling he had, a vibe, that it just wasn't going to be a situation in which he could succeed the way he felt he should, given he was barely five feet tall. He got the sense that I was the only player who mattered to Buchtel. The coaches there also didn't calculate that Little Dru had found a school with a completely different vibe, and a coach so like him it was eerie.

II.

On Sunday nights over at the Jewish Community Center in West Akron, across the street from a vacant tract of woodland that would later be developed into cream-white office condos, a basketball clinic was held by a once-wunderkind college coach whose career had abruptly ended in disgrace. His name was Keith Dambrot, and in 1991, in his early thirties, he had become the head coach at Central Michigan University, a Division I school. It was virtually unheard of for someone that young to be the head of a Division I program and he was making great progress: his recruiting class in 1992 was ranked among the top fifteen in the country. But during a game in 1993 against Miami University of Ohio, in what he said was an attempt to motivate his players, he had used the word *niggers*.

According to court records, he said he had used the term "to connote a person who is fearless, mentally strong and tough," in the same vein that players themselves used the term in referring to each other. At least eight black players on the team subsequently said that Dambrot had always treated them fairly. I believe them, because I got to know Coach Dambrot as well as anybody, and never did I see him act in any way that was racist. It just wasn't in the man.

Regardless of how he had intended his remark, he deeply regretted it. His mother had founded the women's studies program at the University of Akron and had been an inexhaustible champion of equality, so he'd grown up with a strong sense of civil rights. The comment was a lapse of judgment fueled by a competitiveness he could not keep in check. In trying to motivate his team, he had crossed a line.

Scandal erupted once the story broke in the college newspaper. It was soon picked up by the national media, and he was fired in April of 1993. Now, out of coaching more than four years and working as a stockbroker, he was running a Sunday-night clinic at the Jewish Community Center charging a dollar a kid, trying with varying degrees of success to teach them the fundamentals of basketball.

Dambrot took the clinic seriously, like he took everything seriously.

He was one of those compact, intense men who never quite learned where to find the middle ground. There was also no coach in the country who had sunk so low so quickly. He was toxic, untouchable, the JCC clinic a noble but almost pathetic way of maintaining some contact with the game he still loved. He had not lost his fire. He still had it in his blood, and he also had the rare experience of having been a Division I college coach. There was still a tremendous amount he could teach, whatever his status.

Starting as early as seventh grade, Little Dru started showing up at the JCC on those Sunday nights. Coach Dru at the time did not know anything about what had happened at Central Michigan. Dambrot had been recommended to him by another coach, largely because of his college experience, and Coach Dru was willing to take his son to any clinic where he might learn something. Later on, after Little Dru had been going to the JCC clinic on a regular basis, somebody took his father aside and said of Dambrot, "You need to stay away from that guy," because of what had occurred. Coach Dru's basic attitude was that he would find out for himself what Dambrot was really like.

Because Little Dru showed up at the JCC, so did I. I immediately noticed we were just about the only black kids. I also noticed something else. Whenever Dambrot wanted a player to show how a drill should be done, he picked Little Dru. At first I thought it was racist, a white coach always singling out the black kid, some sort of shadow of what had happened at Central Michigan. Then I realized that Little Dru always did it right. That's why Dambrot singled him out.

At those JCC clinics, I also saw how clearly Dambrot identified with Little Dru. They had a player-coach chemistry that I had never seen before and I don't think I have ever seen since. I learned that

Dambrot himself had once been an exquisite athlete who had suffered under others' assumptions that he was too small. Like Little Dru, he'd showed that heart could matter more than size. Gritty didn't do justice to how he played baseball at the University of Akron: in one season alone on the baseball team, he got hit by a pitch eighteen times, willing to do anything to get on base.

Dambrot coached just like Little Dru played—with that classic little man complex. Part of it, I think, had to do with the situation at Central Michigan and Dambrot's determination to coach again no matter what the level. Part of it also had to do with his own family heritage and his feeling that he had failed in the one aspiration in life he had always harbored, which was to be a great basketball player. His father, Sid, had been a member of the nationally ranked Duquesne teams of the early 1950s, and his uncle Irwin had been the captain of the City College of New York team that won both the NIT and NCAA tournament in 1950. His dad kept scrapbooks of their exploits, and Coach Dambrot looked at them over and over, wanting to continue the family legacy. At five-eight he was a well-regarded high school player in Akron, aggressive and relentless. But he wasn't good enough to play in college. He transferred his desires in basketball to coaching. So Little Dru and Dambrot both always had something to prove.

The more he saw Little Dru play, the more Dambrot realized that he had someone special on his hands, no matter how tall this kid was or wasn't. Little Dru's focused, businesslike approach to the game impressed Dambrot, who knew that his kind of intensity was rare in someone not even in high school yet. You never had to get on Little Dru about working hard, like you did with most kids that age. He also had a skill level *better* than that of many college players. Perhaps most compelling of all, he just felt he belonged on the court, was as good as anyone else out there. If so many others were turned off by his size, Coach Dambrot could easily see that Little Dru wasn't the least bit intimidated by it. It was an obstacle that could be overcome the way most obstacles can be overcome—by tenacity, by belief in himself.

Karma entered the scene again. After being rejected for jobs at several local high schools, including his alma mater, something finally popped. In 1998 Dambrot was offered the head coaching job at St. V, a building of low-slung brick that stood as the gateway to the west side of Akron and had that clear-eyed view of the downtown. The area wasn't the best: just up the street at the corner of Maple and East Market was the frowning beige brick of Dominic's Automotive Services. Across the street was the almost-blackened stone of St. Vincent Catholic church, and on the other side was a parking lot. But the school had a strong reputation for academics, and Dambrot was no longer consigned to the no-man's-land of the JCC. He had some place to go, and, in Little Dru, he also had someone who wanted to play for him. "Man, I don't think this is gonna work," Little Dru finally said to me of Buchtel. "I don't think they're gonna give me a chance. I don't think they're gonna give me a chance over there." I shrugged it off, but in the middle of his eighth-grade year, with the high school basketball season having already begun, Little Dru advanced his plan a step further and told his father he wasn't going to Buchtel. Coach Dru first tried to adjust to the shock of it, then tried to counsel him out of it. For one thing, he was *coaching* at Buchtel—how would it look if he couldn't even deliver his own kid there?

"Dru, come on, what are you talking about? We got this all in place. They're expecting you guys to come."

Little Dru said he had made up his mind although he wasn't quite as adamant as he had been in other situations. "You need to talk to Dru," his dad said he urged Harvey Sims. "He doesn't feel like you're giving him a chance."

Coach Dru also offered to resign from the Buchtel job. He said he told Coach Sims, "I'm going to get off the bench because I can't deliver the kids."

"No, you stay," Sims reportedly replied. "I'll talk to Dru, it's early [in the season]. We'll work it all out."

According to Coach Dru, Sims never talked to his son until after the season was over, and nobody among us was committing to Buchtel. All for one and one for all. One thing we did know is that we were bouncing back and forth as eighth-graders, going to Buchtel games, then St. V games, then St. V games, then Buchtel games. It was becoming dizzying.

Harvey Sims didn't know about the unofficial pact we had made, or if he did, he didn't think we would actually make good on it. If he lost Little Dru, so be it—he lost Little Dru. I think he figured there was no way LeBron James, a kid from the projects, was going to go to some Catholic school that was nearly all white and enforced a strict dress code. Now I think he knew we were *serious*, just as I think he also knew that perhaps a mistake had been made in the way Little Dru had been treated at those open gyms. Little Dru went to Arlington Christian Academy, and Harvey Sims went to church there. According to Little Dru, Sims saw him in school and finally asked what the situation was with Buchtel. Harvey Sims said the conversation never took place, but Little Dru remembers it in precise detail. He told Coach Sims that his decision was final: he wasn't going.

When Little Dru announced to Sian and Willie and me that Buchtel was out and he was going to St. V, we at first looked at him like he was hallucinating. This was a major switch, not just in terms of basketball but in terms of social and racial environment. Buchtel was roughly 97 percent minority, with about 40 percent of its 700-odd students economically disadvantaged, which made its academic achievements all the more impressive. St. V was the opposite, with virtually 100 percent of its roughly 550 students going on to college, and a minority population of about 13 percent. Buchtel had a legendary history of athletics in Akron, including basketball. St. V didn't have much history in basketball; its best sport was football.

Yes, we had made a pact to stay together so we could win a national championship. The assumption all along had been that we'd be going to Buchtel, and initially Little Dru's decision threw all of us. Even Little Dru himself seemed taken aback by what he said he had blurted out to Sims. As he later put it, "I just told him that I wasn't going to Buchtel, I was going to St. V. I don't know why I told him. I don't know what got into me." Afterward, he saw Sian, who went to the same school as he did at the time, and told him what he had said, and the look on Sian's face articulated it all: You said that?

"It just came out of me," Little Dru answered.

At first I tried to talk him into coming to Buchtel. But Little Dru was adamant now. We knew we were either going to follow him or go our separate ways, since Willie had always been on the fence a little bit anyway. There were no arguments, but discussions went on for weeks. I thought at one point we really were going to split up. But there were indications that Willie was going to play on the junior varsity as well if he went to Buchtel. Following in the footsteps of Illya, who had gone to a Catholic school in Chicago, he began to think about St. V. He said he spoke to Coach Dambrot, who told Willie he really wanted him if he chose to come. Willie started leaning toward St. V. Then Sian, who was also slated for the junior varsity at Buchtel, said he saw what happened to his older brother, L.C., there. The coach on the Buchtel junior varsity was always belittling L.C.; after the last game of the season, he apparently did it again with Sian in earshot.

"I've had it," Sian remembered saying. "You're not gonna do me like you did my brother." St. V became a possibility for him as well.

Following the lead of Little Dru, we began leaning toward St. V. When he first made the decision, we weren't angry. We just didn't agree with him. I wasn't surprised when Little Dru said he wasn't going to Buchtel. Him being Little Dru, I wasn't surprised by anything he said. But our friendship had traveled a long and sacred road. A pact is a pact after all, and brothers are brothers, if you define *brothers* by love and devotion and loyalty. Little Dru wasn't acting in selfishness. He just wanted a chance to compete for the varsity, and he felt that his relationship with Coach Dambrot, combined with the fact that St. V only had two players returning with significant playing time the year before, would give him that opportunity. He remembered something Dambrot had told him early in their relationship that had always stayed with him: "I put the best players on the floor. If a freshman is even with a senior, I'm going to play the freshman. I'm going to play the freshman because he's got four more years left." Sian and Willie felt they would get a chance to play varsity as well, and I knew I would get my opportunity. So after all the back-and-forth— Buchtel or St. V, Buchtel or St. V—the decision had been made.

Somebody subsequently called the Cottons at home anonymously and told them about the racial incident at Central Michigan. Lee Cotton suspected that the call was coming from someone associated with Buchtel trying to veer us away from St. V, because that's how intense the war over us had become. Lee Cotton had played basketball against Dambrot in high school, and he found the comment totally uncharacteristic of the Dambrot he'd known. Regardless, it would be a lie to say he wasn't troubled. It would be a lie to say we all weren't troubled by what we were hearing, even Little Dru.

Rather than rely on rumors, Debra Cotton ordered the transcripts of the suit that Dambrot had filed against Central Michigan. In it she and her family found the context of how Dambrot said he had used the word. The suit showed that he had not directly called his players "niggers" but said, "You know, we need to have more niggers on our team," in the context of players who are "tough" and "hard-nosed." The suit also showed that he had asked his players for permission to use the word before he said it. "Do you mind if I use the N word?" the court records showed, and several players had apparently said it was okay.

Coach Dambrot, aware of the rumors swirling back and forth, encouraged the Cottons to check out what happened. He took Coach Dru aside and told him about the incident. He also had a player from Central Michigan call the Cottons; he confirmed that what Dambrot had said was meant to motivate, not denigrate, however ill-advised it turned out to be. Dambrot himself was still contrite over what happened. He called his actions "dumb" and "unprofessional." He conceded that the school probably had no choice but to fire him, and the U.S. Court of Appeals for the Sixth Circuit upheld a lower court ruling that Dambrot had not been wrongfully terminated. There was also some vindication: the appeals court agreed with the lower court finding that Dambrot's first amendment right to free speech had been violated by Central Michigan and that he be granted attorney fees.

He knew in his heart he was not a racist.

By the summer after our eighth-grade year, our decision was firm: we were going to St. V. We were comfortable with our choice. Until the doors of the school opened that first day, plunging us into a world we knew nothing about.

6.

School Daze

I.

The four of us may have been brothers to one another. But to many in Akron's black community, we were now traitors who had sold out to the white establishment. They wondered how four talented African American kids like LeBron James and Sian Cotton and Willie McGee and Little Dru Joyce could play at any high school other than Buchtel. Coach Dru felt the brunt of the blame, which only intensified after he left Buchtel to become an assistant at St. V in August 1999, right before our freshman year was about to begin. By that time, we had already decided to attend St. V. But some charged it was all part of a package deal in which Coach Dru was being rewarded for aiming us toward the Catholic school.

Dambrot said that he put Coach Dru on the staff because of what he had done with us on the Shooting Stars. "You've done a great job with the kids, and it would be good to have you here," Dambrot told him. He also figured it would be hard for Coach Dru to simply let go, given the closeness of our relationship with him. Dambrot was right about that, and Coach Dru did have a great rapport with all kids. None of that mattered. He was a marked man, and he went through the agonies of hell, seeing inklings of an Akron far different from the city he thought he knew.

He was coming out of the post office one day when a car stopped at the light. The window rolled down, and a high-ranking official from the Akron public schools angrily called out, "I hear you're pimping for St. V." Coach Dru explained as calmly as he could that his son's decision to attend St. V was his alone, and Coach Dru would honor it as any father should. But the comment bitterly stung because it reflected what many blacks in Akron felt: that Dru Joyce had instigated all this, using his influence over us as a father figure. Never mind that we had made up our own minds alone to attend the same high school together and keep our dream going. The comment also stung because of what he had done with the Shooting Stars. From its humble origins, the Shooting Stars now had eight teams playing in different age groups. The kids on these teams were mostly African American, and kids as young as in fourth grade were getting the chance to play basketball and travel. "To have this guy say this to me after all we were doing for the community—it just hurt," Coach Dru said later. It was the only comment he received directly, but he could see the looks and sense the whispers as he passed by other people.

Lee Cotton went through a similar ordeal. He was hurt as well; he too had been a loyal part of the Akron youth sports community that helped so many African Americans. He too became an assistant coach under Dambrot, only adding to the enmity. Friends he'd known for years were no longer friends, so great was the hostility; people associated with Buchtel had no qualms about bringing it up. "When you coming home?" one Buchtel coach asked Lee and Sian Cotton whenever he saw them. "When you coming home?"

The anger and resentment, Lee Cotton said later, "was from the black community, from my friends, from people I went to school with, even from people I had played with. Just everybody. Everybody." People called him and his son "traitors," and nobody wanted to hear about the mistake Buchtel had made in not giving Little Dru a proper chance. According to Lee Cotton, their feeling was strong and simple: "You're African American, you should go to Buchtel." Others warned Lee against St. V and whites in general: "St. V isn't going to take care of you. White people aren't going to take care of you." Another coach at Buchtel called Sian and told him the same thing: "You're over there with white people. You need to come home. We'll treat you right."

The enmity and antagonism may have reached their peak when Sian was playing in an AAU tournament in Cleveland the summer after his ninth-grade year. He was resting during a break when a man asked him, "You play for St. V, right? You're Sian Cotton."

"Yes," Sian said, and the man shot back, "You're all fucking traitors, and your coach is a pedophile."

"The whole family was considered outsiders by Akron's black community," said Lee Cotton. "We were cast out."

For the four of us, the transition to an overwhelmingly white school carried more than enough of its own challenges. Suddenly there was that dress code to worry about. There were all sorts of rules to follow—being on time, no loitering in the hallways, covering up tattoos in school with long-sleeved shirts and wearing white patches during basketball games that looked like poorly applied medical bandages and often fell off. I didn't know anything about St. V when Little Dru first mentioned it. I didn't even know where the school was. I didn't know it was a Catholic school. I had no impression of the academics. We were just there to play basketball together.

I did know there were a lot of whites at St. V, and I had never gone to school with whites before. I had never hung around white people for any length of time in my life, and I just didn't know how to get along with them. I didn't know what to say. I also had to wait until the basketball season began in December to show the student body what I was really here for.

Starting high school is intimidating, no matter who you are. Everybody looks smarter. Everybody looks bigger. I wasn't scared, but I was self-protective. There was no overt racism, but I did have this feeling of discomfort, as if I truly had walked into a separate orbit. I talked to Maverick Carter, the senior captain of the team; he was three years older than I was, but I had known him since I was five, when I had gone to his birthday party because a friend of my mother's was close to Maverick's parents. I talked to Little Dru and Sian and Willie, of course. There were a couple of white players on the team I talked to, such as Chad Mraz and John Taylor. If you weren't on the basketball team, I didn't talk to you. It was simple as that.

Little Dru felt largely the same way. He spoke to the three of us, and he spoke to other kids who played basketball, but that was it. Nor did other students outside of basketball really talk to him. He had been in racially mixed schools before, but never in a school that felt like this. When he went to religion class, all he saw was "a bunch of white kids." The school had students take communion several times a year, and being Protestant, Little Dru wasn't familiar with the Catholic rite. Instead of kneeling at the appropriate time, he just sat there, and he never went up to receive actual communion. It added to his sense of tentativeness and isolation, and it wasn't until the end of his sophomore year that he felt comfortable enough to talk to other students who didn't play basketball. Until then, he was simply known as "that kid who never said anything."

Little Dru gained a reputation for being snobbish and standoffish. I think it was his innate shyness around new people, combined with the difficulties of becoming at home with the atmosphere of St. V, that made him the way he was. As for Sian, he often thought everybody was against him. He had a kind of militant attitude to begin with. Because he was big he *was* intimidating, and he was convinced that everybody was staring at him. There was no question—heads turned when he walked into the building.

Willie didn't feel the culture shock that the rest of us did: the much bigger shock had been leaving Chicago and going to Akron to live with his brother and go to school there. He'd attended predominantly white schools in fourth and fifth grade, so the racial breakdown didn't bother him. He did worry whether he'd be intelligent enough, particularly in English. He was ultimately classified as learning disabled, which did give him extra time on tests and access to tutors. He still feared that he'd lag behind and be ineligible to play sports, and the blunt truth was that he didn't want to be at St. V if he couldn't play basketball. There was a period of adjustment. In the very first period of his very first class at St. V, a teacher stopped him and told him to tie his shoes, and he hoped he wouldn't get in trouble. There was also the matter of facial hair. It wasn't allowed at St. V. Willie kept getting caught, and would have to make the embarrassing trip to the head-master's office to get the electric razor, then shave in the bathroom. This was too good an opportunity for Little Dru and Sian and me to pass up, to the point where we said he must also be shaving his eyebrows.

Little Dru could have done well in the classroom if he had wanted to. Like the rest of us, he was really only at St. V to play basketball, so basically maintaining the minimum grade point average to be eligible. His two sisters had been honor students, but Little Dru saw school as an unfortunate and obligatory hardship. Sian didn't want anyone to think he was smart. He was also the one who, over time, chafed the most at the school's rules.

I was two grade levels behind when I entered St. V, but it was never hard for me academically. I actually liked schoolwork, one of those students who felt awful when it was time to turn in homework and I didn't have it. I don't know if it was guilt, or just the idea of being singled out, but I just couldn't sit there and say no when a teacher asked me if I had done my work.

There was also the guidance of Maverick, who told me which teachers were comfortable with the idea that we were here to play basketball and which teachers thought it was ridiculous and would pounce if it looked like we were getting any special treatment. He also helped me gauge the attitudes of the students, which didn't take long to figure out. They were either happy with our presence and into the spirit of winning, or they had the attitude, Fuck these kids, why are they here? Coach Dru gave me some simple, effective advice: all I needed to do to adjust was respect other students in the same way that I would expect respect from them.

Overshadowing everything was the fact that some high-echelon figures associated with St. V may not have wanted us there in the first place; their children had come up through the Catholic Youth Organization's sports programs with the expectation of playing basketball at St. V, and now they might not play at all because we were there. One member of the school's board of trustees saw us as ringers who did not belong in a place rooted in academics.

The school, which was a socioeconomic mix of rich, poor, and in-between, took great pride in its history. It stretched back over a hundred years to when St. Mary High School first opened in 1896, followed by St. Vincent High School in 1903. In 1972 the two schools had merged, and since then close to 5,000 students had graduated, guided by a host of advanced placement offerings and honors courses as well as a highly regarded fine arts program. Its mission statement was clear: "In the spirit of the Gospel, we are committed to educate the whole person; to lead and to serve, enlightening the mind, developing the body, touching the heart, and inspiring the soul."

We adopted the dress code, no matter how much it hurt—dress slacks with a belt, shirt with a collar but no name or logo, dress shoes, no facial hair, no braids, no earrings, no visible tattoos, sideburns to ear level only—a *preppy* look on a kid from the projects. Since I didn't own any clothing like that, I had to go out and buy clothes, like it was my first day of kindergarten. We were expected to keep up with academic standards and obey the rules, and gradually we became, as best as we could, part of a world that was initially so alien to us. Along the way we had our moments of imperfection.

Sian and Willie and I played football freshman year, which aided in the transition. It forced us to interact with other students. We were beginning to relax a little bit, make our way through the layout of the three-story building and know which classes were where—English, math, science, social studies, religion. There was a surprising comfort to the school, with its green carpeting covering the hallways and green lockers lining the walls in keeping with one of the school colors. We went up and down the stairway that featured two murals—one of a leprechaun that looked a little bit like Abe Lincoln, and the other a classic Celtic cross with the words *spirit, tradition, honor,* and *pride* written underneath. We discovered the wide space of the Learning Resource Center, with computers dotting the tables and the warmth of its privacy. We found a place to hang out in the second-floor hallway that we called the Block. We began to come to grips with the academic standards. We understood where basketball stood in the pecking order—the locker room, a narrow series of green lockers barely big enough to hold your shoes, made that point. We walked by the wide windowed case that held the gleaming football trophies as sweet as the sun, in homage to the school's four state championships. We were getting by.

Until the first basketball practice.

II.

Based on our experience at the Jewish Community Center, I thought I would be in for a cakewalk with Coach Dambrot at St. V. I thought I was lucky to have such a nice coach. I thought it was all going to be very mellow.

Instead, the firm but patient coach who had held those Sunday-night clinics at the JCC had become a madman, now conducting practices with the same rigor as the Division I college coach that still burned inside him. He made it clear that the program would be run exactly like a college program, that our goal was to win and win big. He told us not to take anything he said personally, that he only wanted to make us better. And then he screamed. He demanded. He cussed. If parents made the mistake of attending a practice, he screamed and cussed even more to make sure they knew he didn't care who was there.

The team's star was Maverick Carter, a six-four forward. He was a natural leader and a superb basketball player, and I know he tried to keep an eye out for us, our mother hen. But Dambrot wasn't about to change.

Little Dru and Sian and Willie and I had been dubbed the Fab Four by a reporter, based on a similar moniker that five freshmen from the University of Michigan had earned when they went to the finals of the NCAA tournament in 1992. I am sure Dambrot hated that. It made us sound cocky. He also knew, though, that even as freshmen we could make a significant contribution, with so few players with experience returning from last season.

He was hard on me, almost ruthless. He believed that perfection was obtainable and would not tolerate mistakes. His eyes were everywhere, never missing anything on the court. During a drill, he would be watching the player handling the ball. You assumed that was the object of his focus. But if you were out of position away from the ball, he was on you. He cracked my game open as if it were worthless, all glitter and no substance, self-absorbed flash and style. I played no defense. I was selfish. I knew fundamentals but snubbed them. I figured at the time he just hated me, thought I was some ghetto-kid hot dog who would never be a team player. I now realize what he was doing, and I'm lucky he was doing it.

Actually, it wasn't luck. It was karma that put me with a high school coach who had been a Division I college coach and had seen players who went on to play in the NBA. His experience told him, even in those early days of my high school career, that I had a chance—*if* I learned how to respect the game and played with the warrior mentality. "I was very difficult on LeBron," he later said, "but in the long run it was good for him. The pressure I felt was that he had a chance to make something great out of his life."

But I didn't see it that way at all.

At least not during that first day of practice.

He was an asshole. There's no other way I can put it. Nonstop screaming for two hours, the kinds of things you would never say to your own children: "Who the hell do you think you guys are, you freshmen! I don't like what you're doing! Sprint! Get back on defense! Get off my court!"

After precisely one day of practice, there was near-insurrection. The way I remember it, Little Dru was looking at Dambrot the whole time like they were about to get into a fistfight, and Little Dru wasn't above fistfighting *anyone*. I was thinking the same thing, only after practice, just jump him in the parking lot. Sian, still filled with the adrenaline of the football season, seemed ready to tear Dambrot's head off. Willie was typical Willie on the outside, mature and keeping it in perspective and, hey, sometimes people turn out different than you think, depending on the setting and the circumstance, and you just learn to go with it. There was also a look on Willie's face that I had never seen before, as if he was trying to believe all those things but was burning inside because he knew what the rest of us knew, which was: Dambrot is insane. All of a sudden Buchtel looked beautiful to us. All of us shared the sickening thought that we had made a terrible mistake.

We were also young. And yes, we were cocky, thought we knew everything about the game of basketball, when the truth was, we didn't really know much at all. Coach Dru had been a great coach, but he was the first to admit that he didn't have the experience that Dambrot had, obviously had never been in the college trenches of Division I. We had never been tested this way, pushed this way, by a coach who saw far more potential in us than we did. He never calmed down during practices. Even if you did something right, you did it wrong. If you made a right-hand layup on the left-hand side, he was all over you for not using the left hand. "That was fucking terrible," he would scoff when we did something he didn't like. "What the fuck is that?" he would hiss. Or "You're fucking up." Or "This sucks." When he called Sian a coward, even though he was one of the toughest players he had ever seen, it was not just to motivate him during practice but to get him fired up if he was ever called that during a game. He had more patience with Little Dru, who uncharacteristically didn't say a word in practice the entire year and just tried to watch, observe, listen, and stay out of the maelstrom.

During the games, Dambrot generally let us play, concentrating his brimstone and fire on the referees, pounding on them mercilessly. I actually felt sorry for some of those refs, because I knew firsthand what it was like when Dambrot breathed his fire on you.

III.

With Maverick Carter leading the way and me starting as a freshman and Sian and Little Dru and Willie coming off the bench, something ignited like beautiful fireworks. We coalesced as a team more quickly than anyone thought we could, and games were easy compared to practice. We started with a 76–40 win over Cuyahoga Falls (for the record, I had 15 points and 8 rebounds in my first high school game) and we just didn't stop. Cleveland Central Catholic. Garfield. Cleveland Benedictine. Detroit Redford. Temple Christian. Mapleton. They all fell, and suddenly we were 7–0.

Then came Central-Hower, an Akron public school with a 6–0 record. The game was a war, as all games against Akron public schools would be because of our decision to attend St. V. We played the game at home. But it felt like an away game, and Maverick Carter had it right when he said, "Everyone in the city, except for our faithful, came here to see us lose."

We started off down 7–3, then Maverick pulled off a 10-point run to help give us a 24–18 lead at the end of the first quarter that expanded into a 43–30 lead at halftime. We turned weak again at the beginning of the second half, and Central-Hower cut the lead to 43–36. Coach Dambrot called a 20-second time-out and made the point in his own subtle style (he screamed) that we had to play better, seal off the Eagles before they made an extended run. We did just that, winning the game by 22 points, 78–56. Maverick finished with 27 points. I had 21 and 6 rebounds. Yet it was Little Dru, in his small frame and floppy-flop shorts below the knee (a sportswriter for the *Akron Beacon Journal* said they looked like sweatpants), who attracted the most curiosity with 3 rebounds, an assist, and a steal.

7.

Swish

I.

Little Dru didn't score any points that day. But he was continuing to develop his shot, and there was no accident in that. He was pushed along by that phenomenal work ethic, which was one of the major reasons Dambrot was relatively patient with him.

After practice he was never the first one to head to the showers. Instead he worked on his jumper. Or challenged Maverick to a shooting contest known as the "W" drill, in which you had to make twelve shots on the move in the fewest attempts possible. Afterward they played one-on-one, even though Maverick was nearly a foot and a half taller than Little Dru. He'd say to Maverick, "Let's go today. You beat me yesterday, but let's go today." And even when he beat

Maverick, it wasn't enough: "You only won once yesterday, I won twice, and I'm going to beat you all three times today." He did it to improve, and he did it to show Dambrot and the rest of the team that, regardless of his tiny size, he belonged on the court.

He was also pushed by his father. They loved each other madly, just as they irritated each other madly. They had trouble separating the father-son aspect from the coach-player part of their relationship. Little Dru had to work almost doubly hard for anything he got, going back to the days of the AAU and the Shooting Stars, when his father would find other players to try out just to challenge him. "I'm about to bring in a strong, quick guard," Coach Dru would tell his son, to see how he reacted and how hard he worked. The purpose was two-fold: to let other players know that Little Dru's starting spot wasn't automatic because his father was the coach, and to make sure he competed every day. "If I got this guy crawling on my back, then I better be at my best every time I'm out there," Little Dru later said.

His father critiqued him mercilessly at times, even when we almost won the AAU fourteen-and-under championship against the SoCal All-Stars. They watched a tape of the game; Little Dru thought he had done a good job on defense, since his opponent had barely scored. In Coach Dru's eyes, his son still hadn't done enough.

"I'm not even getting beaten off the dribble," he protested.

"But your hands aren't active," his dad shot back. "You're not put-ting any type of pressure on the ball."

"Well, what do you want me to do? I'm keeping him in front, and he's not scoring, he's not going anywhere."

Then Little Dru would get defensive and refuse to discuss it any-more. His dad would continue to critique, and Little Dru would find anything else to focus on. He felt so wounded that they couldn't even watch the entire tape of the game together.

During another game in eighth grade, Little Dru kept getting stripped of the ball. He readily admitted that he'd stunk up the gym that day. So, for that matter, had the whole team. On the ride home, Coach Dru put most of the responsibility on his son for the loss. "I wasn't the only one out there," he protested. "You're shouldering all the responsibility on me." Finally he just put his head in his hands; he couldn't take it anymore. Other times he was the one who was on the offensive, refusing to listen to his father during practice, instead challenging him: "Why are we doing this? Why are we doing that?" It reached the point where Little Dru almost destroyed practice sometimes, his competitiveness making him unable to let anything go, pushing his father to the brink. Even when it came to running. The Shooting Stars were expected to make the runs in a certain amount of time, and Little Dru's attitude was his attitude: "I'm not making that time."

Little Dru himself hated losing, even if it was a meaningless scrimmage. In seventh grade, an opponent stole the ball from him and scored the winning point. Since it was just a scrimmage, his other teammates, which included Sian, thought what happened was funny and started laughing. But when they went into the traditional team huddle after the game, Little Dru just reached out and punched Sian in the mouth despite his massive girth and six-three size.

During freshman year at St. V, Coach Dru heard the whispers and so did Little Dru—the only reason he played was due to his father's intervention. Sometimes they were not just whispers. After a scrimmage, an angry parent came up to Coach Dru and pointedly noted how his son had not played very much. "Honestly, your son is a year or two away from making the varsity," Coach Dru responded. "I'm telling you the truth."

The father did not want the truth, followed by the inevitable.

"This is all about your son."

"I'm just being real. You saw how Dru played. You saw how your son played. Say what you want, but your son's a year away."

The anger only festered when his son was placed on the JV. The father stood at practice with a perpetual scowl on his face; following one JV game he tried to attack coach Bob Dezso and Coach Dru had to come between them. Part of the issue was playing time, but the father could not reconcile how his son, despite being taller and stronger than Little Dru, was not nearly as skilled. Coach Dru knew how people laughed freshman year when his son warmed up for games, then were shocked when he actually played, followed by the chants of "midget" and "smurf" and "mascot." Coach Dru just knew that until Little Dru proved himself once and for all, the whispers and the chants wouldn't stop. They probably wouldn't stop anyway. So Coach Dru simply wouldn't accept the mistakes from his son that he would from others.

If Little Dru turned the ball over, it was ten times worse than anyone else turning it over. If he took a poor shot, it was "a terrible shot, how could you do that?" If he fouled, it was a dumb foul. Everything was magnified in Little Dru's case. Coach Dru had decided early on that no one—no one who knew basketball at least—would say that his son got where he was because of being a daddy's boy: "You see it happening all the time with a lot of dads who coach the team, that their son can do no wrong and they just let their son do whatever they want to, but I wasn't going to do that," was the way he later put it.

I would not know anything about fathers bonding with sons in sports because I never had a father growing up. Without being a psychologist, I also know that fathers and sons don't always mix on the court the way they think they will. It is a complex relationship when the father, maybe without quite knowing it, turns himself into a twenty-four/seven coach, and the son, without knowing it, becomes a twenty-four/seven player. I saw that happen to them over the years, even as they both got so much better at what they did. Little Dru was still a demon on the court. He got into more fights than anyone in practice. He fought Sian and Willie and me, and it did not matter if we got the best of him: we understood that he was going to fight back. Clearly he was learning his father's lessons: he could not back down under any circumstances.

After practice was the worst. They rode home together at seven thirty or eight, Little Dru enduring the inevitable rite of a father critiquing every single facet of everything his son had just done, like picking at a scab until it bled. Little Dru only added to the bloodshed with his instinct to question authority.

I would often get a lift home with them. People say I have always had great vision on the basketball court, but I think I had my greatest vision in the back seat of Coach Dru's car. I knew exactly what to do at all times, which was to keep very, very quiet. I like to think I'm a peacemaker and can settle people down. Sports does make tempers flare, and I often crack jokes during practices to keep everybody loose. I knew that trying to *settle* them down, getting them to see each other's perspective, was fruitless. Practice had been hard enough with Dambrot's screaming. For Little Dru, those car rides back home continued the tirade in what seemed like an endless stream, only of what he had done wrong, rarely what he had done right: "You can't accept that you got beat on that play. You can't accept that. It's not acceptable. It can't happen. . . . If it's LeBron and you are going one-on-one with him on a fast break, you've got to strip the ball, you've got to do something: Okay, I got scored on, next play. That doesn't work. . . . Everybody is looking and waiting for the opportunity for you to make a mistake."

Which only made Little Dru tell his father, "I'm tired of listening to it." One of the best days of Little Dru's life was when he got his own driver's license and didn't have to catch a ride home with his dad anymore. Come to think of it, it was one of the best of my life as well.

The bond between them was still powerful. There had been all those days of Little Dru tagging along when his father had played pickup ball at Elizabeth Park. There had been all those days at the house on Greenwood Avenue with Coach Dru rebounding for his son and teaching him. Coach Dru understood that this was his son. But he felt there were times Little Dru needed tough love if he was ever going to realize his dream of playing Division I basketball. Nor was it a matter of Coach Dru's ego trying to overshadow his son. He could care less about his own ego. That isn't why, in the early days of the Shooting Stars, he drove us all over the Akron and Cleveland metropolitan areas just to find us a place to practice. So while it got tense at times, very tense, Coach Dru wanted the best for Little Dru, the very best. Of all the words of advice Little Dru heard from coaches over the years, these from his dad resonated the most: "It is discipline, not desire, that determines your destiny." To Little Dru, those words meant that there is no substitute for preparation. They also meant that when the opportunity arose, wherever it came from, he would be ready to seize it.

II.

We shredded our local schedule that freshman season and coasted into the play-offs in March 2000. But Dambrot had something far more important to grapple with—his mother, Faye, was dying of lung cancer at the age of sixty-six. He began to split his time between the Cleveland Clinic, a hospice in Akron, his full-time job as a stockbroker, then practice. He was exhausted and in terrible grief. To this day, I still don't know how he juggled everything back then. He didn't either, and it would have been understandable if he had just decided to stop coaching for the duration of the play-offs. It was his mother who insisted he forge on; she told him he owed it to the kids who played under him, both black and white.

She died just before the state tournament final four, and the team did forge on. We met her before she died, and she was deep in all our hearts and memories. She *was* a great champion of equality, and for four black kids trying to make it in what was basically an all-white environment, you have no idea how important that was to us, how much it helped us. We played on in her honor.

St. V won the semifinal 63–53 over Canal Winchester, thanks to a

26-point performance by Maverick Carter. It gave us a record of 26–0 and a place in the Division III state championship against Jamestown's Greeneview High School before 13,061 fans at the Value City Arena at Ohio State University in Columbus. I was six-four and 170 pounds at the time, still a little bit gangly, still far away from the six-eight and 260 I would be by the time God was through and said, That's the best I can give, the rest is up to you.

I scored 25 points, but my performance was far from the most impressive one that day. None of us had ever seen anything like what we witnessed; Coach Dambrot said it was perhaps more amazing than anything else he'd ever seen in his coaching career. All I can say about it is this: Coach Dambrot was right. It was beautiful, the most beautiful thing I have ever seen on a basketball court.

THERE WAS NO INKLING of what would happen that day. If there was karma, it was hiding somewhere. Little Dru didn't go to sleep the night before and have some epic dream of how it would all end up. He didn't wake up that morning thinking something special and life-altering was going to happen. That season, he'd gotten about 10 to 11 minutes of playing time a game, his first taste with about 3 to 4 minutes left before the end of the first quarter; since he was small, Dambrot tried to eliminate pressure situations for him and get him open shots. There was no reason to think the routine was going to be any different in the state championship.

The game was in the afternoon, so the team was up by 9:00 a.m. We had breakfast, and because our hotel did not have a full-sized gym, we did our walk-through in the parking lot, going over how we would attack Greeneview's zone defense. We got to the Value City Arena about two hours before game time, which gave us plenty of time to warm up. Little Dru donned his uniform with the number 10 on it, and I put on mine with the number 32 and the "Fighting Irish" insignia across the front.

We weren't nervous as much as we were excited, filled with anticipation, ready to accomplish something that St. V hadn't done since 1984, win a state championship. Coach Dambrot *was* nervous. You could see it in his face as he collected the rubber bands that we liked wearing around our ankles and wrists but weren't allowed to have on during games. He shoved them into his pocket; as the game began he reached inside and fingered them as he paced up and down the sidelines.

Little Dru sat as close to the coaches as possible. He had learned that from his dad: when a coach puts in a substitution, make him see your face first. We weren't playing well at the start. We had no juice. Coach Dambrot almost threw Little Dru to the scorers' table and said, "Go in there and get those guys."

He was greeted by the usual smirks when he appeared on the court. The program listed him at five-two and 110 pounds, but everybody knew that was a hyped-up lie. He couldn't lift a weight to save his life; when he tried to, the weight just lifted him like Popeye before he eats his spinach. Because his shorts drooped below his knees (he said he liked the look), there was always a chance he might trip. Personally, I think he was closer to four-eleven and 95 pounds.

Little Dru didn't feel in the zone when he entered the game midway through the first quarter. The butterflies were maybe more intense now because it was a state championship. Otherwise he did the same as he did every other game—made the right passes, took the shot if he was open.

The first 3-point attempt came from the left corner, with 3:26 left in the quarter. Feet firmly planted for quick release when he got the feed. The ball heaved in a high arc.

Swish.

Little Dru had hit 3-pointers before—in our first game against Cuyahoga Falls he had hit three in a row, so there was nothing terribly unusual about him hitting one here.

The second 3-point attempt came from the left wing about a minute later. A good five feet behind the line. A shot so deep and ill-advised that even his dad couldn't help but blanch. Get a grip, Little Dru. Get a grip. You're not Ray Allen. His defender even got a little piece of it.

Swish.

The third 3-point attempt came with 5:24 left in the second quarter.

Swish.

The fourth came with 4:32 left in the quarter. Six-three defender Josh Carter was fast approaching. But Little Dru released the ball almost as soon as he caught it over Carter's fingertips. Not a single wasted motion.

Swish.

The basket gave St. V a 2-point lead, 27–25. Little Dru was taken out of the game and sat next to his father, who just looked away. He was scared of fiddling with Little Dru's rhythm, so he didn't say a word, not even "Good job." Even with those four straight 3-pointers, the game's television announcers were still dismissive and mocking.

"He looks like he should be playing in a seventh grade game," said one. "Maybe it's a situation where Greeneview just can't find him," said another. When Little Dru came back into the game about midway through the third quarter, nobody was smirking.

The fifth 3-point attempt came with 2:16 left in the third quarter from the right corner. Greeneview defender Joe Pauley running to catch up to Little Dru. His release once again was too quick.

Swish.

The sixth attempt, with 1:54 left, from the same spot. Pauley flying to catch him.

Swish.

All in a row to break the game open, the crowd now in shock and awe. As soon as Little Dru touched the ball they went silent, like the entire world had stopped, and as soon it went through the net they erupted in a roar. I had never seen anybody in the zone like Little Dru was in the zone. Eighteen points in 6 minutes of court time. I just kept staring, and I said to myself that if he made one more 3, I just might have to throw him in the rim, I was so excited for him. This was my *blood brother*, the kid I spent night after night with, the kid I went to the store with, the kid I told everything to, the kid I did everything with.

The seventh 3-point attempt came from the left corner, with 2 seconds left in the quarter.

Swish.

Forget *Hoosiers*, because this wasn't some Hollywood film. This was real. This was *happening*. When he hit that final 3 at the end of the third quarter to give us a 13-point lead, I did lift him in celebration, as if the game was over. I knew it was wrong to act prematurely like that. We still had a quarter left to play. But I was too happy. I loved the accomplishments of my Fab Four brothers as much as my own.

When he came back in, in the fourth quarter, he was fed the ball to try for an eighth 3-pointer, which would have tied the state tournament record for Division III. The crowd wanted him to take the shot. His team wanted him to take the shot. Everybody wanted him to take the shot. Little Dru didn't think he had a good look, so he didn't take the shot. Because that's the kind of player he was even then, utterly disciplined.

Later on, when I looked at the box score, I couldn't help but laugh. I had never seen anything like it before and would never see anything like it again:

ATT	MADE	FG	3-PTS	REB	FOULS	BLK	PTS	MIN
7	7	7	7	0	0	0	21	10

Thanks to Little Dru's performance, we ended up beating Greeneview 73–55 to remain undefeated and win the state championship. He had finally won the respect he deserved, although there would always be players who thought they were better. Coach Dambrot felt vindicated. Coach Dru felt vindicated. He had the best seat in the house, watching his son from the bench. More than that, he knew what Little Dru had been through, all those comments and snide remarks that he had to hear growing up. Across Akron, Little Dru became an inspiration to kids who were small but still yearned to play basketball. They could not relate to someone who was six-six or six-seven. But they could relate to Little Dru. They taped the picture of him that had appeared in the *Akron Beacon Journal* to their walls. They saw him as living proof that size really did not matter.

We were only freshmen, and it seemed like things could only get better.

Then came Romeo.

8.

Romeo Oh Romeo

I.

Five players make up a team, of course, not four, and the Fab Four was just that, the Fab Four. I thought of it as a bicycle chain with a link missing; we needed one more piece to make it whole. The link arrived in the form of a sophomore transfer named Romeo Travis. I was the only member of the team who really knew Romeo, since we'd gone to middle school together. Romeo was a beast on the court when he had the desire, about six-six, tough inside on offense and able to block shots on defense, a perfect complement to Sian. At least he *seemed* perfect, until I remembered how much trouble I had with bicycle chains as a kid.

When that chain holds together, when everything is smooth, it just runs and runs and runs. But if one little link slides off, your chain just pops and you can't get where you want to go. I could see that Romeo might be the missing link, or the link that popped.

Romeo had gone through a falling-out at Central-Hower as a freshman. He said a basketball coach he was quite close to left the school; then he made a stupid quip that a teacher interpreted as a threatening remark, and the principal of the school said it would be best if he did not return. He had to find another school. I began to work on him to come to St. V, and got the other members of the Fab Four to buy in. Sort of. Maybe. We were tight, maybe too tight, almost cultlike in some ways, so well did we know each other at this point. "He was coming on a new team, and he didn't know anybody," Willie observed later. "He had to take care of himself. So that was his demeanor when he came in, he had to look out for himself. He still wasn't one of us." Combine that with the personality of Romeo, a self-admitted smart-ass who had trust issues and sharing issues and thought the Fab Four giggled and carried on like little girls. Even before he got to St. V, there were issues. He didn't like Little Dru because he felt that Little Dru, in going for a steal during a scrimmage in middle school, had scratched him in the eyes on purpose. He didn't like Sian because he thought that Sian acted like Little Dru's bodyguard and made himself out to be a bully. Shortly before Romeo came to St. V, he played in a summer league game with Sian and Little Dru. I wasn't there and Sian was just having fun, playing point guard and shooting 3-pointers and feeding the ball to Little Dru in the post. They won handily, but afterward Romeo was angry and upset.

"Man, what's your problem," said Sian. "You always got a problem."

"You're just out there shooting the ball."

"It's only a summer league game. It doesn't even matter. And we won by thirty."

"I don't care. You should have passed me the ball."

"I'm tired of you acting like that. I'm about to beat your ass right now. Square up. Let's go."

"No."

"Let's go. Let's fight right now."

"I'm not coming here. I'm transferring. I'm going back."

"Then get your ass out of here. We don't even need you."

Romeo softened up toward Willie pretty quickly, but even they'd had a war of words over who had outperformed whom in a middle school basketball game. There was an issue over a girl. Right from the outset, it was a difficult mix. As Romeo said later, "I didn't want to be there, and they didn't want me there."

Part of Romeo's trouble in getting along was his upbringing. His parents had separated when he was about two, and he and his three siblings were raised by their mother, Carolyn. When he was a baby the family lived in the Elizabeth Park projects, and I knew what that was like because I had once lived there. If the kids went out to play, Carolyn had to go with them just to see what was going on, keep them away from the drugs and the shootings. The family moved to San Francisco for a year, then came back to Akron for a little bit, then to Canton for two years, then back to Akron. Carolyn's sister moved in with her at various times, giving them a total of eight kids to watch after. They lived in whatever places they could afford when Romeo was young (I knew something about that too)—a house on Cuyahoga Street where the kitchen light never worked and the floor flooded, another one on Lake Street, where the pipes were also bad, in a neighborhood that was rough. The family lived in an apartment complex in East Akron that had more than its share of fighting, little gangs battling for turf. Romeo was too small to be involved. But his oldest sister, La'Kisha, born five years earlier and fearless and in many ways his greatest protector, got into scraps all the time. At another point, the family lived in another complex in East Akron that Romeo described as a "little hell," a strip of small and cramped apartments in an alleyway off of Arlington Street.

Carolyn worked where she could to help make ends meet—as the head cashier in a department store, at Kmart, on the line at a soap factory, as a manager at a gas station. She was on welfare on and off, because even when she worked, it wasn't enough to care for the family. She had to take food stamps. Sometimes he and his siblings ate three hot dogs three times a day, hot dogs and rice for breakfast, hot dogs and beans for lunch, and then anything to disguise the fact that it was a hot dog for dinner. There were other staples in the house such as fried chicken and hamburger, but Romeo and his siblings were desperate for variation. La'Kisha, the oldest, would go to a grocery store and on different occasions steal such items as spaghetti and steak and Stouffer's lasagna just so they could have something different.

Like me, Romeo went to a variety of schools growing up. He moved constantly, about twenty times. But I had found Little Dru and Sian and Willie. They were my body and soul; they kept me going no matter how tough the times. Romeo never had that, the concept of lasting friendship silly and wasteful in his eyes. "You could be my friend today, and you could be gone tomorrow," he would put it.

Something happened to Romeo when he was twelve or thirteen

that shows how his sense of distrust developed. One summer day, he remembered, his father called and said he was coming to see Romeo. His friends asked him to play hoops or just come over. Romeo said no, because his dad was coming, and he so rarely saw him. His mother warned him not to get his hopes up. She advised him not to wait. But Romeo knew his dad was coming, he just knew it, and he waited all day until finally, at 9:00 p.m., he gave up.

At a young age, Romeo developed a protective shield of self-interest. His uncle had taught him, "You gotta get your own." Romeo took that lesson to heart even in elementary school, buying four-packs of the snack Jell-O for a dollar and selling them at school for fifty cents a pop to make a tidy profit. He could have cared less whether other kids saw him as a bum trying to hustle some money, or maybe someone who actually had pretty good marketing instincts. He had no use for us, and he made that clear. He knew another kid at St. V already, and as far as he was concerned, that was all the friendship he needed. Nor would he share Twizzlers and Starbursts and pizza and soft drinks with the rest of us, our unspoken rule. That was for idiots.

His mother, Carolyn, thinks she might have contributed to that selfishness. With the older kids pretty much off on their own, according to Carolyn, she became interested in her own life and doing what she wanted, like going out at night and clubbing. She felt guilty about leaving Romeo. She knew she should be spending more time with him, so she began to give him gifts to reduce the guilt. "I just gave him stuff to take my place," she later said, and Romeo would cling to those possessions and refuse to share them with anyone else. "He just wanted to hold on to [possessions] because I think he thought that's all he had, just stuff," said Carolyn. "So he became selfish for a very long time."

She also believes he became angry as a teenager, disappointed by his father, disappointed in her because she wasn't there for him. As La'Kisha put it, "He was left to his own devices."

He also wrestled with the difficult transition from a public high school, where he never took a book home and was late to school over fifty days, to a private Catholic school where he was suddenly expected to work—science projects, study hall from three to five before practice, "all sorts of crazy shit," in Romeo's words. He actually could be charming when he wanted to; at Central-Hower he used this charm to his advantage, putting his arm around a teacher, asking her how her day was, coming in early and acting like he needed help. At St. V, Romeo said, "that shit didn't work. There was no point in trying."

Romeo was smart and could easily handle the academics at St. V if, as his mother said, "he put his mind to it." But she said he missed a lot of days of school. He just didn't want to go until he was told he would be placed on academic probation and, in the words of his mother, "not be able to play if he didn't get it together." He went to school, doing enough to be eligible.

Then there was the dress code, when he was used to sneakers, jeans, and a T-shirt. At first, he begged his mother every day to let him return to public school. Between homework and basketball, Romeo was getting up at seven in the morning and not getting home until eight thirty or nine at night (unless it was a day where Coach Dru picked him up at 6:00 a.m. for a before-school workout). The approach to basketball at St. V was vastly different, and more challenging than what he was used to—so much so that he didn't even make it through the first practice. But his mother had a no-quit rule; no matter how unpleasant it was, you weren't allowed to give up. That certainly applied to St. V. He was staying, no matter how much he whined and complained.

To Little Dru, there was something suspect about Romeo's attitude, a deliberate effort to be different from the rest of the crowd. It seemed to him that Romeo got upset just to get upset, went on rampages because somebody had innocently asked him a question he didn't appreciate. You could ask him anything, and if he didn't like it, his response would be, "Who the fuck are you talking to?" He and Little Dru got into it all the time, on the court and off. Little Dru was a yeller on the court: if Romeo did something he didn't like, he was immediately in his face, his admonitions laced with curse words. Romeo's role at the beginning wasn't particularly hard as far as Little Dru saw it: make rebounds on defense, make layups on offense. He had trouble finishing, and if there was anything Little Dru could not stand, it was a teammate missing a layup. Perhaps the greatest puzzlement to Little Dru was that Romeo refused to dunk even though he was six-six and a great athlete.

If Little Dru felt like practice needed to be more intense, he would purposely hit a player with a cheap shot. If a player set up a screen, he wouldn't go around him but straight through him. One time Romeo hit Little Dru with a cheap screen, and Little Dru answered back by shooting him a little elbow. Romeo started talking trash, warning Little Dru there was going to be trouble if he did it again. Little Dru did it again, this time hitting him in his balls. The play ended. Another one began, and Romeo came down the court and punched Little Dru in the face. Romeo, in turn, thought Little Dru was a "little arrogant dickhead" who talked like he was the head coach. Yo, shut up, you're the smallest guy out here, Romeo thought to himself.

Even Romeo admitted that he went out of his way to be an asshole, starting something called the Rude Association, whose purpose was to hurt other people's feelings with cuts and digs. Romeo was an expert at that: he could size you up instantly, had a knack for pointing out the characteristic you most despised about yourself. If you were small and self-conscious about it, he was sure to focus on that. If he spotted someone wearing a hat in the hallways of St. V, he'd announce, "That's the dumbest fucking hat I've ever seen." If someone said, "What's up?" he responded, "Screw you." He said in front of white students, "Too many whites at this school." Romeo liked to call himself the "angry man." Willie, who had a kind word for everybody, readily acknowledged that Romeo was an asshole, but at least an equal-opportunity asshole: he was nasty to just about everyone. But Romeo, while he may have been loath to admit it, was also lonely. The Fab Four was tight, and Romeo felt he could never penetrate us. "They don't like me," he told his mother. "They don't want to be my friend." She said he just had to give it time, but Romeo couldn't see the light of any improvement.

"I'm by myself," he answered back.

Romeo's transfer from a public high school to St. V only intensified resentment from Akron's black community. Again, a Catholic school was poaching a player who belonged at a public school. Some in the St. V community were also upset by Romeo's arrival; they saw him as another ringer who would deny playing time to other kids on the team who might not be as good but still deserved to play.

Those deserving kids would be riding the bench more than they might have been in the past because Coach Dambrot was on a personal mission of redemption. He knew the best way to do it was to win back-to-back state championships at St. V, and if that meant that certain kids never played, then certain kids never played. He paid virtually no notice to them during practice, until they got the message and just quit. Dambrot also spiced up the schedule, reducing the number of local teams and increasing the number of high-profile opponents from out of state. If the Fab Four had a dream of a national championship, I think Dambrot had his own dream of making it back to the college ranks. It might be impossible, given what he had been through, but at the very least he needed to prove that he was a great coach.

II.

We started the 2000–2001 season exactly the way we had ended the one before, by continuing to win. Cape Henry Collegiate was one of Virginia's top teams, with two players who'd already signed scholarships with Division I schools. We overpowered them 74–38. Next was Wisconsin powerhouse Case High School. We beat them by 52 and put on a 30–6 run in the second quarter. We beat the Redford Huskies from Detroit, one of the ten best teams in the Midwest, 45–40, thanks in large part to a 5-point surge by Romeo in the fourth quarter. For all his huffing and puffing and moaning and groaning, Romeo could come through when he wanted to. Then Cleveland Central

Catholic: 78–63. Poor winless Crestview: 74–31. Always gritty Massillon: 84–51. We moved to a a 9–0 record and climbed to number three in some of the national rankings.

Next came the biggest game of our lives, against Oak Hill. If we beat them, we probably would be ranked number one in the country by *USA Today*, the measurement that everyone uses to determine a national champion in high school basketball, since there is no such thing as a national play-off. If we could run the table the rest of the way, go undefeated, maybe the dream of a national championship for the Fab Four Plus One would be ours as *sophomores*.

We didn't beat Oak Hill. We lost 79–78, and of course we could have won had I made that last shot. Coach Dambrot still heaped lavish praise on me that night. "He played a great game," he told the *Akron Beacon Journal*. "Everything we did was because of him." I still cried after that buzzer sounded, those feelings roiling inside me that I had failed my brothers, placed our dream in jeopardy. Karma? Bad luck? Which one was it? For one of the few times in my life, I didn't want to know.

The tears soon stopped. The Oak Hill game had given us the confidence that we could play with anyone at any time, and we sliced through the rest of the regular season. Rayen from Youngstown, 98–40, where I hit for 20 and Romeo 25. Traditional Catholic school rival Walsh Jesuit—done and gone, 96–37. Then came another local war.

FOR THE FIRST TIME since the Fab Four made its fateful decision not to attend Buchtel, we are playing them. To accommodate the crowd, this game is being played in the James A. Rhodes Arena at the University of Akron with its seating capacity of 5,500. Because bragging rights are in the offing, more than four thousand people have shown up. Buchtel supporters and Akron's African American community—many of whom still see us as traitors—have come out in droves. As Little Dru says later, it's like playing with a "bull's-eye on your back," the atmosphere is so intense.

It also adds to the sense of challenge and adventure. Little Dru, for one, likes being in hostile territory. We all do, since it makes victory even more marvelous. The only problem here is that Buchtel, despite a relatively mediocre season, is ready to play at the end of January in 2001.

Harvey Sims truly does know what he is doing. In one game his team scored 129 points, but here he puts in a slowdown offense. It takes our rhythm away—we always play up-tempo, a high school version of the "forty minutes from hell" that the Arkansas Razorbacks became famous for when they won the national championship in 1994. We are frustrated. They are squeezing the life out of us. We are bothered and the crowd is feverish as they begin to sense upset.

A 12–2 run by Buchtel closes our lead at halftime to 33–27. The third quarter comes, maybe the worst quarter we ever play together as members of the Fab Four Plus One. We score exactly one basket. Buchtel scores 10, taking the lead with Charlton Keith's slam dunk at the end of the quarter, 37–36.

Is it possible that we are actually going to lose?

After being stymied without a basket in the middle two quarters, I hit for 2 at the beginning of the fourth. Then Romeo hits for 2 and the lead is back in our hands, 46–40. Buchtel's Keith responds with a 3-pointer, closing the gap to 46–43. But we have a sense of rhythm now, and even with those bull's-eyes on our backs, we escape with a 58–50 win.

WE FINISHED WITH A RECORD of 19–1. We buried the competition in both district and regional tournament play to once again advance to the Division III final four at the Value City Arena in Columbus. We had a slight scare in the semifinals against Wayne Trace from Haviland, pulling out a narrow 56–50 victory. In the finals against Miami East from Casstown, a team with a 25–2 record, we started out tight, throwing up air balls. Miami East shot out to a 17–8 first-quarter lead and even led at halftime, 26–25. In the second half we found our extra gear. The final score was 63–53 before 17,612 fans, the largest to ever see a state tournament game in Ohio.

What had seemed unimaginable two years earlier, when we were scared freshmen appearing in front of a coach who made Darth Vader seem affable and easygoing, had now happened: we had won back-to-back state championships. We also finished fifth that year in the USA Today poll. I was not only getting bigger, growing to six-six, but thanks to Dambrot I was getting better, appreciating the intricacies of the game. His constant pounding drove me to do what he hoped I would do: I was learning how to respect the game. Even then, as a sophomore, hype was starting to encircle me. There were quiet rumblings that I would go straight to the NBA from high school, a notion that probably had been promoted the most by then General Manager

Jerry Krause and his special assistant B. J. Armstrong of the Chicago Bulls. They had been at the game against Oak Hill to scout DeSagana Diop, who would become the first-round draft pick of the Cleveland Cavaliers straight from the prep school. But as they watched me play, they started scrambling through their programs. Who *was* this number 23 from some school in Akron called St. Vincent–St. Mary, hitting 3s and making assists and playing the passing lane and, despite the likes of Diop and Carruth and Edelin, being the best player on the floor that day? At first they thought they had discovered a senior gem that nobody else had noticed. They found out instead I was just a sophomore. Their hearts sank a little bit, but it was the first game in which I got major attention at the professional level, particularly after Krause and Armstrong started telling other NBA general managers. Opposing players, just after competing against me in games, asked for my autograph. People were scalping tickets for fifty dollars apiece. Coach Dambrot began to feel a little bit like he was touring with Elton John. Back in Akron, the phone began to ring constantly about me, and he had trouble getting any work done in his regular job as a stockbroker. I was being touted as the best sophomore in the country, until Dambrot dismissed the comment as usual as if he was spitting out chewing tobacco: "Best sophomore in the country, my ass. You don't even play defense."

How good could I really be? I had no idea, although I knew I was improving. But Coach Dambrot, despite making sure I didn't get a big head, did. He had coached three players who had gone on to play in the NBA, and while he wasn't about to tell me this, he thought I was better than any of them at the age of fourteen. No matter how much he rode me and criticized me, he thought I was perhaps the most coachable player he had ever encountered: he only had to tell me something once and it stuck. Dambrot still had contacts in the college ranks, so he called a former colleague named Ben Braun, then the head coach at the University of California, and invited him to watch me play. Dambrot just wanted to make sure what he was seeing wasn't some apparition. Braun accepted the invitation and made one comment afterward:

"That kid won't ever play in college."

While Romeo and the Fab Four were having enough issues to fill the couch of a family therapist for days on end, Romeo proved he could work with us on the court with an 11.8 average, even though he didn't start a single game. Sian, no matter how much his heart belonged to football, was becoming more and more of an enforcer on defense, our resident bully, the basketball equivalent of the bouncer at a hot club, unafraid to set up screens and take charges if it enabled others to score. We even gave him a nickname because it seemed so appropriate—the Brawl Street Bully. Willie, still adapting to the effects of the operation on the separated shoulder that he had originally suffered in football, came off the bench without complaint. Little Dru's high-arching 3-point balloon kept getting better and better.

We still didn't know what to do with Romeo, shower him with love or just dump him in the shower. He was still on the outside looking in. He still thought we giggled like a bunch of girls, and we still thought he was the most selfish human being ever created. On the court, we tried to put aside the differences between him and the Fab

Four. He had now savored a state championship with us, and I think he shared our desire for something more. At least until we were on the bus on the way back to Akron, when he whined that he was going back to Central-Hower. We knew he never would, but that was our Romeo.

9.

The Invincibles

I.

As we went into our junior year, our dream of a national championship was in its fullest bloom.

The schedule was stronger. I was putting on some facial hair now, looking more and more like a man than a still-awkward kid, playing with more and more physicality. I had grown to six-seven, and Little Dru came up close to my knee now at five-seven (just kidding, Little Dru. It was my waist). It wasn't our growth plates that mattered. It was our continued togetherness off the court that translated to on the court. The four of us had played together for so long that we could virtually get out there blindfolded and know exactly where each of us was. So how could the dream possibly fail?

Coach Dambrot wasn't coming back.

He is certain he told us directly. But the recollection of Little Dru and Romeo and me is different: we remember finding out through a reporter and feeling devastated. Given our relationship, how much we had done for him, and how much he had done for us, we just assumed, based on our recollections, that we would be the first to know. Little Dru was probably stunned the most, because he and Dambrot were so close. He also felt Dambrot had just used the team to get back into college coaching, revealing a side of him Little Dru had never realized before.

Dambrot had been offered an assistant's job at the University of Akron, and he was taking it. He had gotten what he wanted, his ticket out of disgrace to possible redemption, not to mention he was bored to tears as a stockbroker. He had been out of college coaching for eight years, and he had paid more than enough for an admittedly terrible mistake. He said later it was one of the hardest decisions he ever made, and even his own son barely spoke to him for several weeks. He knew that we had resurrected a career that had "crashed and burned" because of the Central Michigan bloodbath; he was indebted to us for that. But he felt he had to prove to the outside world that there was such a thing as coming back from adversity, and he believed that the only opportunity to coach in college again would come from Akron. I will not lie about how I felt at the time—scorned and deceived. Another adult had broken a sacred promise and run out on me. Later on, as life made me wiser and I learned how hard it is to get a second chance, I would understand that Dambrot had no choice. When I was sixteen, I felt as if Dambrot had betrayed me and the rest of the Fab Four. He had even betrayed Romeo, who'd let himself feel that

Dambrot might help him achieve his potential more than any other coach ever had.

I never wanted to talk to Dambrot again, never wanted to see him again. And when I did see him, I refused to call him "Coach." Instead, I called him "Mr. Dambrot," just to show the depths of my resentment.

Sian took the news with angry bitterness. "He used us. That's exactly what it was. He used us to get back to college. . . . He didn't have any loyalty. He had no loyalty and he sold us up the river, and there's no getting around it. And he was dead wrong."

Little Dru was equally emphatic. "I didn't care about his personal reasons at all," he later said. "I just know what he had said to me, that he was going to be there for four years. What came into my mind was 'Man, you lied to us.' You just lied."

Little Dru's emotions would became even more complicated when rumors started circulating that his father would be taking over as head coach. He was proud of his father, and whatever they had been through, he had always wanted to play for him. But everyone on the team had seen how rocky their relationship was—how hard Coach Dru was on his son, and how hard Little Dru took his father's pressure and fought back against it. If Coach Dru took the top job, we could only see the hard times between them getting harder.

Like the rest of us, Coach Dru was completely surprised by Dambrot's departure. He was looking at prospective homes for sale in Akron with his wife, Carolyn, when a sportswriter from the *Plain Dealer* of Cleveland called and told him.

Later that evening Coach Dambrot himself called and shared his reasons. This did represent a once-in-a-lifetime opportunity to get back into college coaching. According to Coach Dru, Dambrot also shared another concern that had contributed to his decision to leave. Given the hype that had begun to build around me, the increasing feeling that I would go straight to the NBA from high school, perhaps even be a possible lottery pick in the draft, Dambrot worried that he could no longer control the situation. The possibility of agents hanging around like gnats. The possibility of shoe companies offering me under-the-table endorsements. The possibility of reporters trying to dig up dirt. (Just for the record, there was no major scandal. I never took a dime from anyone.) Dambrot believed he could not afford the risk of being involved, even indirectly, in any scandal, since his college coaching career already had a major strike against it. He told Coach Dru he had been advised by a college coach he respected that he should leave before anything erupted: "My goal and my dream is to resurrect my college coaching career, and I've got to get out of this thing."

He told Coach Dru something else: "I want you to take over. I'll support you with the board at St. V, and I've already had a couple of preliminary conversations. Those are your kids. You brought them to me. They'll play hard for you, and I'll support you in front of the board."

It had always been Coach Dru's own goal and dream to become a high school coach. But now that the dream was within reach . . . he wavered. He wasn't sure if he was ready. He worried that, as much as he had learned from Dambrot, he still didn't have enough practical experience at the high school level. He worried about the junior-year schedule, which pitted us against eight teams that hovered around the top twenty-five in the country. He worried that the team was moving up from Division III in Ohio to Division II, which would also step up the competition we faced. He worried that he couldn't prepare us well enough for the steep challenges before us. He worried that, whereas Coach Dambrot had been a new voice to us at St. V, he was an old voice because of all those days we had spent with him on the Shooting Stars, and that familiarity would inevitably breed contempt. He even asked us if we wanted to play for him. He worried about living up to fans' sky-high expectations for the team (some had already made their reservations in Columbus for the state tournament). He saw the job as a no-win situation: if we took the state championship for the third time in a row, or even won a national championship, it would be because Coach Dambrot had molded us. If we lost, it would be Coach Dru's fault because he'd squandered our talent through his inexperience.

He worried and he fretted. It was his nature to be careful and methodical, and he expressed those worries and frets to his wife.

"Dru, how can you say no?" Carolyn answered. "This is God honoring all those years that you have been with those guys. All those times you drove up and down the highway." She was referring to the Shooting Stars' early days, when Coach Dru would drive Sian and Little Dru and me all over the place just to find us a gym for practice.

Coach Dru knew she was right. He thought about all the sacrifices he had made to give a bunch of kids from Akron a chance to play basketball at the highest conceivable level. When he was offered the head coaching job at St. V, he took it. The selection process took about a week, and during that week word spread that the Fab Four Plus One were going to transfer. Little Dru did not think his father would get the job. He just didn't think that St. V, a prestigious school that was predominantly white, would make a black man the head coach. Plus his father wasn't Catholic. He hadn't come up through the ranks. The Fab Four Plus One didn't know what was going to happen, and it was Little Dru who suggested we leave and go somewhere else, maybe to Buchtel, maybe to Firestone. There was talk I might go to Oak Hill, play out the season, and afterward challenge the then-existing NBA rules so I could declare for the draft as a high school junior. Once Coach Dru had been selected, the first African American head coach in the history of St. V, there was no way any of us were going anywhere. "This is a dream come true," Coach Dru told the *Akron Beacon Journal* when he officially took the job. "It's something I've been working toward since I got into coaching."

His wife was right: this was God's way of honoring Coach Dru's years of dedication and sacrifice. And God was surely leading all of us somewhere.

II.

We had gone 53 and 1 our first two seasons. We had won two state tournaments and had finished our sophomore season ranked in the top ten nationally. Our biggest problem, besides Coach Dambrot's screaming, had been the ongoing tension with Romeo. He still relished the role of I-don't-need-anybody, although it was hard to tell if Little Dru was right and it was a facade. Did he want to be a part of us? Did he not want to be a part of us? Did we as members of the Fab

Four want him to be a part of us? Did we not want him to be a part of us? The relationship between Little Dru and Romeo had thawed somewhat. They became friendly, but, as Little Dru later put it, "I knew at the end of the day he might just lose his mind and blow up and go crazy." And getting a Twizzler out of him was still impossible; he'd look at you as if you were trying to rob him.

But Romeo could score in the post and was explosive. He had a quick jumper. He could rebound, and we all knew that he'd be even more of an asset to the team in the coming year. Now we really did have a legitimate shot at the national championship.

We opened against Avon Lake, the result a 41-point blowout, 81–40. I scored 28 points and had 7 rebounds, and have to confess I did have one favorite play, a blocked shot that rocketed out of the gym. But Romeo was the star that night. He scored 16 points in 14 minutes. Sian, playing his patented defense, helped hold Avon Lake to just 5 points in the second quarter to give St. V a 47–17 lead at halftime.

The game set us up for our first major challenge of the season, against Germantown Academy, a private school in suburban Philadelphia that had been ranked fifth in the country by *USA Today*. Germantown had three Division I signees in the six-six Matt Walsh (Florida), six-seven Lee Melchionni (Duke), and six-eleven Ted Skuchas (Vanderbilt). We were no match for them in size, which is probably why *USA Today* had ranked us sixth.

Sian, now up to 285 pounds, with amazingly quick feet for some-one that big, was just a beast on defense. Along with Romeo and senior forward Jermeny Johnson, the team more than held their own against the Germantown frontcourt of Melchionni and Skuchas and six-six forward Alex Lee. Skuchas fouled out early in the fourth quarter with only 5 points, and Lee had only 3. Melchionni got his points, 19, most of them were from the perimeter. I did my job offensively with 38 points, and Little Dru added 11.

Germantown was tough to the end. They made it a 5-point game, 61–56 with 3:07 left, after Matt Walsh hit two free throws. But we had the advantage of a friendly crowd, since we were playing at the Rhodes Arena in Akron (all of our home games had been moved there to accommodate larger crowds and bring in more revenue to St. V, since it seated 3,900 more fans than the school's own gym). We also had the advantage of a sweet 3-pointer by senior guard Chad Mraz right after Walsh's free throws that closed the game and led to a 70–64 win.

There was no letup. The next opponent was Vashon High from St. Louis, ranked seventh in the USA Today poll and a reigning state champion. Its star player, six-four swingman Jimmy McKinney, an early signee at the University of Missouri, had confounded Buchtel the year before with his dunks and jumper.

We played flat in the first half, but more than our flatness signaled danger. We played without emotion, coasting really, putting it on when we felt like it, not putting it on when we felt like it. We weren't the scrappy underdog anymore. Based on the success of the last two seasons, we had become the team everybody desperately wanted to beat. More and more fans, even on our home turf of Akron, came to watch us lose. Vashon moved out to a 27–19 lead at halftime as we struggled from the floor, and I committed five unforced turnovers.

Coach Dru made adjustments during halftime. I was switched to point guard to get more into the flow of the offense. The rest of the team came out of its tiredness. We turned the ball over only twice. I scored 15 points for a total of 26 for the game, while McKinney fouled out late in the fourth quarter with only 9 points. Little Dru made a 3-pointer with about 3 minutes left, to put us up by 44–39, and that was the end of it, a 49–41 win.

Ho hum. Big deal. St. V beats another nationally ranked opponent. We were that confident. We were that cocky. The sneaker wars over me were also escalating, meaning piles of equipment for everyone. The team got full sponsorship from Adidas, which for the players included travel bags, four or five pairs of shoes, uniforms, two or three warm-up suits, personalized headbands, and winter coats. The shoes I got were custom-made with my number, 23, and the initials "LJ" imprinted on them. It was another reason to feel full of ourselves. But as long as we were winning, what difference did it make? If people wanted to turn us into arrogant victors, let them. If people thought we were too cocky, let them. If people wanted us to lose because we were no longer the bunch of nobodies from Akron, let them.

For Romeo, the favorite part of the game occurred before the start when he walked into the gym. Right away he could tell what kind of team we were playing, the way some opponents turned their heads and would not look you in the eye, the way some others had that starry look as if they were saying, Oh my God that's them, the way others tried to stare you down and act macho. But none of the poses mattered to Romeo or the rest of us, because we knew what was going to happen right at tip-off.

We truly were invincible. Nobody could beat us.

10.

The Invincibles?

I.

Early that season, we kept winning. But the wins were ugly, "smoke and mirrors," as Coach Dru called them.

After the close call against Vashon, we easily beat highly touted Louisville Male from Kentucky, 90–69. Then we played Roger Bacon from Cincinnati; they had us, jumping out to a quick 10-point lead. We narrowed it to 60–59 after three quarters, largely because three of their starters got into foul trouble. So we were lucky. The game moved to a 66–66 tie with 3:42 left. Then Little Dru, fearless and confident and inspirational as ever, hit a crucial 3-pointer to give us the lead, 69–66. We finally started forcing some turnovers, which got us to the free throw line. The General came through again. He hit for six free throws in the last minute and seven seconds, to close out a 79–70 victory that was far tighter than the score indicated.

Although we had beaten teams from Ohio by narrower margins, the game still felt like the closest we'd ever come to losing against another team from the state. Many also thought it might be a foretaste of the state championship in March, which meant we had a significant challenge if it came down to that. Unlike our two previous opponents in the state championships, Roger Bacon would not fall easily. But there was plenty of the season left to play, and predicting opponents in a state championship was a fool's game anyway. Would we get there? It was a given, with the talent we had. But would they? That was their problem.

What the Fab Four Plus One did know was that we had basketball games to play, and we weren't playing them as well as we could—a 3-point win against Detroit Redford undecided until the final minute, a 7-point victory against St. Benedict's from Newark, New Jersey, in which we were down by 12 in the first half and needed 15 from Romeo in the second half to pull out the win.

Coach Dru fretted about our defense. He thought it was sloppy, and he was right. But it was more than just defense. Something foul was brewing and building up. Something of our own creation. Coach Dru warned us that we were off-kilter. But we were invincible. We were still ranked fourth in the *USA Today* poll. And when you are invincible, the last thing you do is listen to good advice.

The Fab Four Plus One respected Coach Dru. We loved him. But the dynamic was different now. As an assistant, he was the coach who consoled you after Dambrot chewed you out over some minor mistake during a drill. Now Coach Dru was *Head Coach* Dru. His relationship with some of us had started close to seven years ago. We did truly see him as a father figure; that wasn't necessarily a productive relationship for a coach to have with his players. Dambrot put the fear of God into us. Coach Dru showered a role model's warmth upon us. It makes for a great man, but it doesn't necessarily make for a great coach, particularly when you have teenagers who have discovered the ultimate freedom of the driver's license.

"We were straight up disrespectful to Coach Dru," Sian would later admit. He was right. We were still stuck on Coach Dambrot. As angry as we were at him for running out on us, we still wanted him as our coach. We were still primed to respond positively to his in-your-face style, to his frequent insistence that our performance was "fucking terrible." Coach Dru was different. He definitely wasn't laid-back. But he never used obscenities and wouldn't tolerate them from us. His approach was more genteel, and we couldn't get the father-figure image out of our heads. He was the guy who had driven us down to Cocoa Beach for that first AAU national tournament, not the man who could coach St. V to a third straight state championship. He was the man who mentored us during the summers, not the man who could drive us through a schedule of top-ranked opponents that took us as far away as Delaware and Trenton. I saw Coach Dru as a substitute teacher, and everybody who has gone to school knows how it is with substitute teachers—you never do a thing they say except talk back and argue and ignore. We also had an easy escape if we didn't win another state championship. As Sian put it, "We had already won two state championships, so if we failed, it was his failure, not ours." Sian and Coach Dru were having other issues as well. To tell the truth, Sian didn't get along with any of the coaches; even with his own father, Lee, Sian would fall into a surly funk. Only Willie was consistently respectful, because Willie always was able to put things in better perspective than the rest of us.

We never really took into account the pressure Coach Dru endured from all sides. The St. V faithful automatically expected another state championship. Others at St. V were upset that he'd been named head coach because he was considered an outsider. Some in the black community wanted him to lose because the Fab Four's decision not to attend Buchtel would forever be unforgivable.

Soon after Coach Dru took the head coach's job at St. V, he received an anonymous letter warning him not to ever think he could be part of the St. V family. He felt there was an underlying racism to it, and he believed that it represented the beliefs of many people, his outsider status as a black man. He felt constantly scrutinized, to the point where he said the team was not allowed to wear black sweats sent by Adidas because it wasn't a school color. He also said he got flack for the team wearing black practice uniforms, even though the name "Irish" was in school colors. He was damned if he did, damned if he didn't—everybody was coming at him from every angle—but we didn't understand. Or we didn't care to understand. Because we were still undefeated. We were still invincible.

II.

The Slam Dunk to the Beach tournament in Lewes, Delaware, which took place over the Christmas break in 2001, was the mother of all high school basketball tournaments. The promoter, Bobby Jacobs, paid out over $100,000 in transportation costs, according to the *Akron Beacon Journal.* He also paid another six figures in hotel and meal expenses to attract thirty-four teams from twelve states, eight of which were ranked in the top twenty-five. In return Jacobs got dozens of major sponsors, including $75,000 from the state of Delaware, so I'm guessing he made a nice profit off of all of us. The economic impact on the Lewes area, a Delaware shore town normally sound asleep in the winter, was said to be about $3.5 million.

Such tournaments were becoming the national rage, making high school basketball feel far more professional than it should have been. Athletic directors and coaches of top-ranked programs spent hours on the phone with tournament organizers discussing promotional fees and expenses. Looking back on those negotiations, I think they were too much. Coaches should be coaching, and athletic directors should be athletic-directing. The interest of promoters was self-interest—their goal was to make money off of us. For all the hype enveloping us, we were still just high school kids.

But since we were still in high school (I actually turned seventeen during the tournament), we didn't give any thought to these excesses at the time. I just knew that more than thirty of the nation's top one hundred seniors were slated to be at the tournament, which meant that dozens of college and pro scouts would be there as well. It was a great place for St. V to showcase its skills, particularly if we were going to make our push toward a national championship in the *USA Today* poll. A strong showing here would probably move us up a couple of notches, energize us after a string of lackluster games in which the Fab Four Plus One all knew we could have played better. Intensity was missing. Our defense *was* porous. We hadn't heeded Coach Dru's warnings. He continually told us that if we kept it up, somebody would come along and smack us down when we weren't expecting it. But we were also 6 and 0.

Our first game of the tournament was against St. Benedict's, yet another ugly win. It was clear that we were still seeking our rhythm, just as it was clear that we were still hungering for Coach Dambrot. If we had to practice defense all night, that's what he would have somehow made us do, because that's the kind of coach he was. Coach Dru was more benevolent.

And then in our next game of the tournament we played Amityville High School from Long Island.

AMITYVILLE IS NO SLOUCH. They are defending New York State champions in their division and have a bona fide All-American in six-nine senior center Jason Fraser, who will later go on to play at Villanova. They have won 34 out of their last 35 games. But we have won 60 out of our last 61. We start out well, moving to a 9-point lead in the second half. Most of our opponents quit at that point. Amityville refuses to give in, backed by the play of Fraser, who will score 28 points for the night and take in 18 rebounds.

They go up by 5 with just a few minutes left, but pressure-time 3-pointers by Romeo and Little Dru keep St. V in it.

Then a basket by Fraser and a free throw by teammate Max Rose with 15 seconds left gives Amityville a 3-point lead, 82–79. The game is over.

But not yet.

With 5.4 seconds left, I hit a 3-pointer while getting fouled, and convert it into a 4-point play to gain us an 83–82 lead.

A time-out is called by St. V. Coach Dru lays out a strategy for how he wants the team to set up pressure on Amityville on the inbound. We have never done it that way before and we aren't about to do it now because we think we know better. We don't let Coach Dru control the huddle, and his son makes it clear we aren't going to follow his instructions. But our stubbornness backfires. Little Dru gets beaten, and on the inbounds pass Amityville guard A. J. Price breaks into the clear. I foul him, which gives him two free throws. He makes the first.

83–83.

He makes the second.

84–83.

We manage to get the ball down the floor for one final shot.

The ball is fed to me. I split two defenders.

I get the look I want from about twenty-five feet, sweet and open. And here we go again, déjà vu upon déjà vu, slow motion upon slow motion. The shot is clean off the fingertips. The rotation is good. The angle is right. This is it. This is it! An 86–84 win at the buzzer to give me 42 for the game.

C'mon, baby. C'mon! In or out? In or out?

Out.

We have lost. We are no longer invincible.

THE REACTION TO THE PLAY Coach Dru laid out in that final time-out against Amityville was yet another signal of where our heads were at, the eternal cockiness. Coach Dru himself realized he wasn't coaching as much as he was handling egos. He placed the onus on himself for not controlling the huddle, but he was upset that we had not listened when he was, after all, the head coach. Instead, we had continued to think we knew more about the game than he did and ever would. We still didn't get it.

We were 7 and 1, with some pretty nice notches on our belt. We were damn good, and we knew we were damn good. When the season resumed, and the quality of competition dipped a little bit, the games seemed almost boring—22 points over the University School, 40 points over defending state champion Franklin from Pennsylvania, 33 over Brush. As Romeo later put it, we expected to win by 25 or 30, so when we won by 25 or 30, what was the big deal? His attitude was still a continued source of aggravation and concern. His transition to St. V had been brutal, and although he was getting closer to us, he wasn't one of us. He still threatened to return to Central-Hower, and Coach Dru had to talk him out of it: "Why go back there? For what? Why would you leave this?" So Romeo stayed, feeling like the puzzle piece that would never fit in, jammed into a spot that didn't have the right shape.

By the time Oak Hill came up again, we were 15 and 1. But our behavior was just getting worse and worse. Practices became contentious. There were constant squabbles. We would have scrimmages, and instead of playing, all we would do was argue over calls Coach Dru made—fouls, travels, out-of-bounds, you name it. The arguing would completely disrupt the scrimmage, which would completely disrupt the practice. Other times we just clowned around.

One day Little Dru got mad at me because he thought I was shooting too much. So he started launching 3s of his own. Romeo, exasperated, threatened to leave practice if Little Dru did it one more time. Which of course Little Dru did. Which of course resulted in Romeo leaving practice. Another time, Coach Dru ordered us to run because we weren't practicing hard enough. We refused, and he had no choice but to cancel practice. Yet another time, Romeo used four obscenities and was ordered to do a hundred push-ups. He did about ninety before he just quit, and another player stepped in to do the rest. Beyond the breakdown in practices, the team just never seemed to come together. We had the Romeo situation with the continued threats to quit. We had another player who had transferred in and never blended. There was also another player who was brilliant during practice but then didn't compete hard during games.

Coach Dru now had a mutiny on his hands, and he didn't know how to quell it. He kept telling us we were going to ruin our season. He kicked Romeo out of practice five times. Because he didn't allow cursing, he made us do those push-ups. But given the mouth of Dambrot, we found it almost amusing. Instead of maintaining his position as the head coach, Coach Dru too often sank down to our level and bickered with us. It made no difference: even Willie thought we could win with or without Coach Dru.

More and more, Coach Dru began to find the season unbearable. Most coaches at the high school level got to make mistakes in the anonymity of small gyms before small crowds. As the legend around me and St. V continued to grow, he made his mistakes in front of television cameras in a sold-out college arena. Whatever he did was being dissected by more eyes than most high school coaches ever had to face in their career, much less the first year of their career.

Before the season had started, Coach Dru had gone to a basketball clinic at Kent State University. One of the speakers was a coach who had experience at both the college level and the pro level. He gave out two pieces of advice: first, when you go into a new job, you fire everybody on the existing staff; second, make sure parents know their place. Coach Dru dutifully took notes, but he didn't listen. He paid for it. Even when St. V did win, Coach Dru barely had any time to enjoy it before a steady stream of parents appeared in the almost cell-like sparseness of his office, with the green cinder block walls and the green radiator and the beat-up brown La-Z-Boy recliner and the desk of institutional gray. They bluntly asked him, "How come my son didn't get to play?" Parents of seniors seemed particularly incensed: "Isn't this supposed to be about the seniors? Shouldn't my kid be getting a shot?" Coach Dru felt that even assistant coach Steve Culp, who had wanted the head job, was making things difficult. When parents approached Culp about playing time for their sons, he said to them, "I don't know why. I don't have an answer." Coach Dru strongly felt that Culp, instead of commenting at all, should have sent the parents directly to him as the head coach.

Coach Dru tried to explain that this wasn't the Shooting Stars anymore, where some parents, as a result of their son's association with the team, expected preferential treatment. He tried to dissuade parents from the belief that you could put any four players on the floor with me and still win. But that's what parents believed, and that's what they wanted. Even the victory against Germantown Academy, one of the five best teams in the country, had been marred by complaints. He came home that night, and instead of seeing him smiling, Carolyn saw the ashen face of a man who felt he just could not win on any level.

He also knew he had made some mistakes. Right before the season began, he called senior Chad Mraz on his cell phone on the way to work and told him he was going to start as the off guard, but that Little Dru would be the point guard. He wanted to put an end to the controversy up front, and Mraz had missed his entire junior year because of a torn anterior cruciate ligament. He later acknowledged it wasn't the right thing to do: he just should have let the competition between the two play itself out. Instead he perceived tension between Mraz and Little Dru going into the season, and once again there were the inevitable whispers that Little Dru was getting preferential treatment from his father. Even some parents of sophomores were saying that their sons were as good as Little Dru and should be playing.

Coach Dru and Little Dru, both feeling pressure, continued to butt heads. Players were just waiting for Little Dru to do something wrong. They were all bigger than Little Dru. They were all more athletic. So Little Dru, as usual, still had to find a niche, which he had done all his life. He took charges. He handled the ball well, and he handled the pass. He could shoot. The one thing his father couldn't tolerate was turnovers, because that's what separated Little Dru from the other players who wanted his minutes. Little Dru was also human. The second he made a mistake on the court, even fans reacted by groaning, "He shouldn't be playing." Which led to his father's now familiar refrain of perfection:

"You can't be good. You have to better than all of them. You have to be great."

"Dad, I'm trying. I can't make a mistake?"

"No, I'm not accepting mistakes. You can't make a mistake."

There were times that Little Dru felt so much weight that he cried. There were times when he became hesitant on the court, lost his instincts and his confidence in what he should do because of the fear of doing something wrong. He worried that the fear might become ingrained in him, until he realized that he had to play aggressively— "Let the chips fall where they may," as he said later.

Since Dambrot was coaching at the University of Akron, he still came around from time to time. He watched us practice, and he could tell that we had lost our killer instinct. He was convinced that it had nothing to do with the coaching change, but with the success we had experienced during our first two years: success of the sort we'd had as a team could actually wear down our unity, as each member started to crave more individual accolades. Dambrot believed he himself could have done no more to prevent that kind of selfishness than Coach Dru could have. We weren't scared freshmen and sophomores anymore, but juniors with rapidly developing minds of our own. We knew what we were doing. Our record seemed to prove us right, as we continued to rack up easy wins leading up to the Oak Hill game: East Liverpool by 28. Walsh Jesuit by 43. Buchtel by 25. Hoban by 25.

The prospect of another game against Oak Hill pumped the adrenaline. *USA Today* had ranked them fourth in the country with a 25-and-1 record; we were ranked number five with a 15-and-1 mark. Our 1-point loss to them the year before still stung. After that game, Oak Hill's coach Steve Smith had dismissed us as a good JV team. I was personally fired up by the impending face-off between me and Carmelo Anthony, who had transferred to Oak Hill from Towson Catholic High School outside Baltimore and would go on to become a star with the NBA's Denver Nuggets.

At the USA Youth Development Festival in Colorado Springs the summer before, featuring the forty-eight best high school players in the country, I had roomed with Anthony and seen him play. I had come back to Akron and told my teammates about this guy from around Baltimore who was good, really good, the best player I had seen at the festival.

Our game against Oak Hill was on the same day as the NBA All-Star game in Philadelphia that night, and various pro scouts and executives came to the Sovereign Bank Arena in Trenton to watch the tangle between Carmelo and me. I guess we put on the show they wanted—dunks in traffic, steals off the dribble, sweet and soft ten-footers, 3-pointers. Together we combined for 70 points—I had 36 to his 34—and I was named Most Valuable Player. I took the MVP trophy back to apartment 602 of Springhill, which was all the way to the right on the top floor with an unobstructed view of the St. V football stadium, adding it to the collection I'd gathered over the years. I went back to my room decorated with the posters of Jordan and Bryant and Iverson. I didn't really care about the award, since we'd lost to Oak Hill 72–66.

Granted, Oak Hill not only had Carmelo Anthony, but at least six other players who were Division I recruits at universities like Wake Forest, Miami, and Cincinnati. Maybe that was why the rest of the Fab Four Plus One seemed cold—even a little intimidated. I tried to pick it up offensively, but I just didn't do enough by myself. It was our second loss in a row to Oak Hill. It was also our second loss of the season. But we could still rationalize it—hey, we'd been beaten by the best. Despite the cold shooting from my teammates, we had played respectably. We had kept it close, pulling to within 3 at one point. So even that loss didn't change our attitude very much. Then all hell broke loose.

11.

Cover Boy

I.

My notoriety was expanding among those who followed high school basketball. I was getting more and more accolades, but I still thought it was just another magazine cover. I had already been on the front of several, and *Sports Illustrated* wasn't widely read in the Springhill apartments. A reporter named Grant Wahl hung with me for a couple of games, and the photo shoot in the St. V locker room felt like it took hours. Not to mention the grief I got when they decided to put mist all over my face so it looked like I was sweating. They did it over and over, and even Little Dru, as he watched, thought to himself, This is crazy.

The cover was dated February 18, 2002. Looking back on it, the attention it received for someone just a junior in high school is still hard to fathom. In one hand I was holding a basketball that had been given a yellowish tinge so that it looked like a shiny sun. I held my other hand in front of me, fingers spread wide as if I was halting traffic. A green headband clung to my forehead, my lips puffed with arrogance. I liked the image at the time. I was seventeen years old.

In hindsight, I also know they crafted it for their own purposes, a high school basketball-dunking duck-for-cover bad boy, at odds with who I really was. The cover title was "The Chosen One," and the line beneath it said, "High school junior LeBron James would be an NBA lottery pick right now." I was mentioned as the next possible heir to Michael Jordan, as a *junior*, in *high school*. The article noted that the shoe wars had become increasingly competitive, with Sonny Vaccaro, the famed Adidas rep, hosting my mother in Los Angeles, and the normally reclusive Phil Knight, the cofounder and chairman of Nike, doing the same in Oregon.

In the article, NBA general managers seemed to be competing to see who could come up with the most complimentary quote. They compared me to Magic Johnson, as ridiculous at the time as comparing me to Michael Jordan. Danny Ainge, the former coach of the Phoenix Suns, said if the choice were his, he would make me not simply a lottery pick but the number-one pick of the NBA draft. Ridiculous again, given my age and true stature. The article failed to acknowledge how little high school greatness really means. What if I got hurt? What if I wasn't tough enough? What if it turned out I really wasn't good enough? What if?

Even worse, I thought, was the failure to highlight the people who had been so integral to whatever success I'd had so far—Little Dru, Sian, Willie, and Romeo.

Maybe naively I didn't really understand what it truly meant to be on the cover of *Sports Illustrated*. I took it in stride. As Willie later said, none of us really understood just what impact it would have, how big it would be. The cover pushed me onto the national stage, whether I was ready for it or not and whether my team was ready for it or not. Coach Dru understood, because it didn't take long before there were as many as thirty reporters at our games. On top of all the other pressures that weighed on him, he now had the burden of a player who, like it or not, had become a celebrity. St. V headmaster David Rathz, sensing the potential of chaos, had at the beginning of junior year closed the institution to the media during the school day. Before the ban, cameramen were filming me in the classroom. I was being followed around by sneaker representatives. I had trouble eating in the school cafeteria in peace, as did other students tired of cameras lurking there. Rathz knew it would only get worse if nothing was done. Some members of the media were shocked by the ban: the headmaster had no qualms. "I would rather be blamed for being hard-nosed and strict and uphold our academic standards than turn it into a circus," he said later.

After the *Sports Illustrated* cover came out, Coach Dru now faced a similar dilemma, since practices were held after the school day. A stream of followers was beginning to emerge, Coach Dru realizing quickly that they were jockeying for position over my future. They acted like they were interested in Coach Dru, "cheesing in your face," as he called it, telling him what a fine job he was doing. Coach Dru could tell they had no interest in him, that he was just a conduit to me. It seemed like everybody wanted to be around. He recognized few of the faces, and closed practices to outsiders.

Coach Dru had already gotten a taste of the maneuvering over me during a St. V football game in the pouring rain in which I was playing. A man came over to Coach Dru and talked like he knew him, though Coach Dru did not have the faintest idea of who he was. They chatted about the game, and then toward the end he handed Coach Dru a packet and said, "Hey, just pass this along." It wasn't until he got home he saw what it was—a proposal from an agent.

What had made us so great was the way we had played as a team. That is what had brought us two consecutive state championships. The *Sports Illustrated* cover had made us all into rock stars, only reinforcing our sense of our own invincibility junior year. In the classroom some of the Fab Four Plus One also began to flout the rules. Little Dru showed up late to class and then wised off. Sian ultimately stopped doing his homework, or would just copy it from someone else. When he took tests, he had a cheat sheet, and one time he got caught. Sian always sat in the back of the classroom, and one of us would walk by the classroom and say Sian's nickname, Si, and he would sneak out the back door without a hall pass. "We were getting away with murder," Sian said. "And that's a lot of the reason why a lot of the teachers in the school didn't like us. And the students felt like we were getting away with murder." Jealousy was also building, fellow students who did not appreciate the notoriety that a group of kids were getting for simply being basketball players. But we didn't care, since it was a small minority.

"Everybody was in on it, from kids to teenagers to our peers to students in the school to the administration," said Little Dru later of the lavish attention we received. "It was like, We can do this and nothing's going to happen. We can do anything." I was arrogant, dubbing myself King James; my head did swell. In hindsight I should have kept quiet, but I also was what I was, a teenager, and every reporter in the world seemed to be rushing toward me at once.

As for the season, we had lost a couple of games, which meant that the dream of a national championship would escape us junior year. There was no way *USA Today* would ever rank us number one with those defeats to Amityville and Oak Hill. Yet we were strangely untroubled by that. We would still win the state tournament. We would still win our third straight state championship in 2002.

Weeks passed, but still the cover's impact did not dissipate. I was hounded for autographs wherever I went. Adults wanted the magazine signed. So did kids, and I tried to accommodate all of them, until I figured out that parents were sending their kids in so they could then sell the signed copy on eBay—weirdly similar to the drug runners who used children as their mules. Little Dru and Sian and Willie and Romeo were all stopped for autographs as well. None of this adulation helped our attitude on the court; we still argued during practices. We still didn't listen to Coach Dru and his assistants, Coach Cotton and Coach Culp. As freshmen and sophomores, we had often stayed late after practice to hone our skills, be the best we could possibly be. Now, with our own cars, we cut out right after practice was over. As Little Dru later said, "We lost our work ethic. We lost our focus. We lost our sense of urgency."

We partied harder and harder, because that's what stars do, isn't it? Instead of going to bed early the night before a game, we stayed out late. Romeo, of course, was the one who ultimately put it in the sharpest focus, since there was no such thing as a party he didn't like: "We were sixteen- and seventeen-year-old kids partying like adults, staying out until four or five in the morning when we had games the next day at three. We were doing things we had no business doing because we just figured we'd wake up and win." Romeo chased more than his share of girls, and in his designated role of "party animal," used fake identification cards to get into clubs.

Coach Cotton became so frustrated with us that he thought about quitting. He never would have done it out of deference to Sian. He never would have run out on his son like that. But he wasn't enjoying his job anymore. He hated going to practice and seeing all the petty fights. He hated our loss of intensity. He even hated the warm-up music we listened to out loud before games—Jay-Z, Ludacris, Snoop Dogg—with its references to "bitches" and "hos" that in Cotton's view were morally wrong. It wasn't a basketball season anymore. It was a circus. Now ESPN was there. Now the national networks were there. Now the network affiliates from Akron and Cleveland were there. Like Coach Dru, Coach Cotton hated what we were doing to ourselves and what was being done to us.

Coach Dru still warned us; we still ignored him. We saw the consequences of our sudden stardom in our very first game after the cover story appeared. We were playing George Junior Republic in a sold-out Beeghly Center at Youngstown State University before 6,700. The kids who went to George Junior, in Grove City, Pennsylvania, were tough; they'd been sent there to be straightened out. It was a residential school for disadvantaged youths, and on this day at least, they played basketball with the same kind of toughness that put them in George Junior to begin with. The game was rough, too rough. I was getting hard-fouled all over the place as I drove to the basket, and the referees refusing to call any of them intentional fouls. My mom was in the stands, and after one particularly egregious foul, ran onto the court and had to be restrained.

The fouls just kept coming, and I did something I learned never to do again—I retreated to my jumper instead of just continuing to drive to the hoop. I hate to say it, but I guess I was tired of getting beaten up. We had a 33 percent average from the field, including 5 for 29 from the 3-point arc. We combined for 14 points in the third and fourth quarters. I scored 20 points, my second lowest total of the season. If it weren't for Chad Mraz's 11 points and Romeo's 10, we would have been finished. Instead we were tied 50–50 at the end of regulation.

Little Dru opened the overtime with a 3-pointer to give St. V a lead, and we thought we were safe. But a foul shot by John Brown tied the game, followed by a 3-pointer from Tyrae Denmark. We lost 58–57 in overtime, marking the first time that the Fab Four had ever lost two games in a row since seventh grade.

Then, the worst of all possible things happened: we started winning again.

Orange by 11 at the Canton Memorial Field House with Shaq in attendance to see what all the fuss was about. Central-Hower by 8 after building up a 20-point lead. Firelands High School from Oberlin by 60 in the sectionals of the state tournament. Hoban by 39 in the district semifinals. Then Central-Hower by 5 in the district finals.

We just kept on rolling.

Warrensville Heights by 29 in the regional semifinals before a crowd of 20,532 at the Gund Arena in Cleveland, the largest crowd ever to see a high school basketball game in Ohio. Scalpers were selling tickets for as much as two hundred dollars apiece. St. V's allotment, 3,500, sold out in three hours. I know that many came out to see me that day, the afterglow of the *Sports Illustrated* cover still shining brightly. But the real star was Romeo, who despite his don't-mess-with-me personality (his nickname was "Grimey" by then) scored 31. Ottawa-Glandorf by 19 in the regional finals before a sell-out crowd of 8,788 at Toledo's Savage Hall, in which Romeo again scored 31.

It put us into the final four. There, on the other side of the bracket, loomed Roger Bacon, a Catholic school with the nickname Spartans spread across the front in script. Was a rematch in the finals inevitable? Of course it was, but there would be no close call this time, where we simply got lucky. This game would be different.

We knew Roger Bacon would be physical, just like they had been in December. We knew they were bigger than we were. Now it was March, and we knew exactly what we were getting into this time. As good as Roger Bacon was, we had still beaten them. We were on the right side of that 79–70 final score; we didn't focus too much on how much closer that game had been than the score indicated. As for the three losses during the season, we could explain those easily: Amityville had the crowd going for it; George Junior Republic played the game like tackle football, and the refs, who were from their home state (because they were nominally the home team), didn't call a thing; Oak Hill was Oak Hill, with all those Division I recruits. In other words, we had an excuse for every one of those losses.

We were ready. And we showed the depth of our preparation for the state finals the night before the game.

For some reason that Coach Dru will never figure out, officials at St. V put the basketball team and the cheerleaders on the same floor of our hotel in Columbus. Battling a terrible flu and shivering with the chills, he could hear the cavorting and carrying-on in the hallway

The Shooting Stars twelve-and-under team in 1997. Top row to the farthest left: assistant coach Lee Cotton. In front of Cotton to the farthest left: me. Second row to the farthest right: Coach Dru Joyce II with Sian Cotton next to him. Front row to the immediate left of trophy: Little Dru Joyce.
PHOTO BY DEBRA COTTON

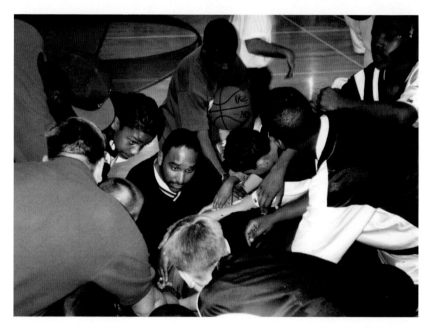

Coach Dru in the middle of a huddle for the Shooting Stars during the qualifying tournament in Columbus for the AAU nationals in 1997. I'm all the way to the right leaning on Sian. The team qualified for the national tournament in Salt Lake City and finished tenth.
PHOTO BY DEBRA COTTON

The original Fab Four during freshman season at St. V in 1999–2000. From left to right: me, Sian, Willie McGee, and Little Dru. PHIL MASTURZO/AKRON BEACON JOURNAL

Little Dru cutting down the net after a crucial win freshman year. Despite his small size, Little Dru's competitiveness was such that he got into more fights than anyone else on the team.

PHIL MASTURZO/AKRON BEACON JOURNAL

I celebrate with Little Dru during freshman season after he completes one of the most remarkable performances in the history of Ohio high school sports despite being barely five feet tall.

PHIL MASTURZO/AKRON BEACON JOURNAL

Romeo Travis in his hotel room sophomore season after the first of three epic battles against the greatest dynasty in all of high school sports, Oak Hill Academy. Well over a hundred Oak Hill players have gone on to play Division I basketball and more than a dozen have played in the NBA.

PHIL MASTURZO/AKRON BEACON JOURNAL

Little Dru being comforted by Romeo Travis during a heartbreaking last-second loss junior year.

PHIL MASTURZO/AKRON BEACON JOURNAL

Future NBA star Carmelo Anthony and I shake hands after St. V played its second game against Oak Hill, this time as juniors. I had 36 points and Anthony 34. The game attracted NBA scouts and executives from all over the country. PHIL MASTURZO/*AKRON BEACON JOURNAL*

Here I score 2 of my 36 points against Oak Hill, then ranked the number one team in the country. PHIL MASTURZO/*AKRON BEACON JOURNAL*

I read the cover story about myself in *Sports Illustrated* in February 2002. The story catapulted me into the national spotlight at seventeen and had an enormous impact on our team.

PHIL MASTURZO/*AKRON BEACON JOURNAL*

Keith Dambrot, who coached St. V freshman and sophomore seasons before leaving to become an assistant at the University of Akron. In the 1990s, he was one of the youngest Division I head coaches in the country at Central Michigan, until his career there ended in disgrace.

PHIL MASTURZO/*AKRON BEACON JOURNAL*

Sian cradling a distraught Little Dru in his arms after a shocking defeat junior year.
PHIL MASTURZO/AKRON BEACON JOURNAL

The group who would come to be known as the Fab Five at our junior prom. Left to right: Willie, Sian, Little Dru, me, and Romeo. PHOTO BY DEBRA COTTON

Coach Dru, who became head coach of St. V after Dambrot left, in a game against Columbus Brookhaven senior year. Both teams were ranked in the top ten nationally, and the game featured an almost make-believe finish. PHIL MASTURZO/AKRON BEACON JOURNAL

Fans mobbing the St. V bus hoping for my autograph senior year after I had just appeared on the cover of *ESPN The Magazine*. The media explosion was such that I was asked to appear on the *Late Show with David Letterman*, *Live with Regis and Kelly*, and *The Oprah Winfrey Show*. PHIL MASTURZO/AKRON BEACON JOURNAL

Sian and I are laughing with each other in the late stages of a 54-point victory senior year against Willard High School. The game was played in front of a sell-out crowd at the University of Akron's James A. Rhodes arena. We also had sell-outs in Los Angeles, Philadelphia, and Trenton. PHIL MASTURZO/AKRON BEACON JOURNAL

Romeo sprawled out on the infamous Hummer that my mother bought me senior year, leading to intense controversy. It was just one of a series of battles that St. V and I fought with the Ohio High School Athletic Association. PHOTO BY PATTY BURDON

Romeo dunking the ball against Detroit Redford senior season. After transferring from another school his sophomore year, Romeo was initially so disliked by the Fab Four that he thought about leaving. PHIL MASTURZO/*AKRON BEACON JOURNAL*

Coach Dru conducting a phone interview when St. V traveled to Greensboro to play R. J. Reynolds High School senior year. The game drew more than 15,000 fans, a record for a high school basketball game in North Carolina. PHIL MASTURZO/AKRON BEACON JOURNAL

The Fab Five on Senior Night in January 2003. Because the team was such an enormous draw, the game was the last played at the St. V gym, which had limited seating capacity.
PHIL MASTURZO/AKRON BEACON JOURNAL

The Fab Five on our graduation from St. V. From left to right: Romeo, Willie, me, Sian, and Little Dru. We would never play ball as a team again, but we will always be brothers. PHOTO BY PATTY BURDON

into the early morning hours. Eventually, he emerged from his room, furious that we would be acting this way the night before a state championship against a team that, unlike most of our opponents, didn't fear us. Coach Dru scared the cheerleaders half to death as he hollered them back into their rooms. The assistant coaches were nowhere to be seen. He looked each of us in the eye and questioned our hearts and our character.

We knew he was right, so we listened. We nodded. We did all the things teenagers do when they've been caught. Coach Dru went back to bed. And we still partied, just a little bit more discreetly. Sian didn't go to sleep until 4:00 a.m., even though the championship would be played a mere seven hours later. Romeo snuck out of the hotel at one point. Even sweet Willie and his roommate sneaked girls into their room. Little Dru and I weren't little church mice either. Because the game was so early, we had to wake up between 5:30 and 6:00 a.m., and we'd put in our food orders the night before at Max & Erma's restaurant in Columbus to get a decent breakfast. But we were exhausted.

It only got worse when I woke up with severe back spasms. Immediately, I knew that even if I could play—and I had no idea if I could—I wouldn't be close to a hundred percent. I knew that my sudden torment was karma coming back around; the payback for our attitude was finally coming due. I had been perfectly fine the night before, not a hint of pain. I had never experienced back spasms before. I had never missed a game. We had just played the semifinals the day before, and I hadn't done anything that would explain them—hadn't come down hard or landed wrong. Now the biggest game of the year was several hours away, and I could barely walk.

Karma.

I managed to struggle out of bed. I was taken to the medical center at Ohio State. There, they tried to loosen my back muscles with one of those machines that send electrical impulses beneath your skin. I felt better—until just before game time, when my back cramped up again. I could move, but my range of motion was limited. I still wanted to play, and Coach Dru faced a dilemma: leave me on the sidelines of the Value City Arena and let me stretch and try to get warm, or put me in the game with the hope that I would start to loosen up and feel better. He decided to play me.

II.

First period begins before 18,375 fans, yet another state tournament record. There are 121 seats for the media, all of them taken.

Opening tip to Little Dru. Brings it upcourt. To Romeo off a feed. Takes a fifteen-foot jumper from the right side for the first shot of the game. No good. But Romeo isn't worried:

> *This is my second state championship. It's just business as usual, go ahead, kick some butt, and go home. I didn't even think twice, because we had beaten them previously. We know these guys, so it's nothing. Just another notch in my belt.*

Rebound by Roger Bacon. They turn it over. Little Dru upcourt again. Feed to me. I score on a little runner from the left side. 2–0.

Like Romeo, I feel no fear:

*We knew we had a game against them the next day, but
who cares? We're still winning most of our other games by
40. We can get away with it. We're St. Vincent–St. Mary.
Nobody can mess with us. I am so confident of victory that
I publicly promise it in a press conference after the semifinals. I know it's the kind of quote that is immediately pinned
to the bulletin board of the Roger Bacon locker room, but
a fact is a fact. We played you earlier in the year at Kent
State, and it was a close game for a little bit, but we ended
up pulling away at the end. Hey, we beat you already. We're
definitely going to do it now. They're a predominantly white
team with a few black kids. How can they beat us?*

Bacon's Josh Hausfeld, a six-three guard on his way to Miami of
Ohio, in the lane to the hoop. Tied 2–2.

Turnaround jumper by Romeo off the glass. No good. Still 2–2.

Then Bacon's six-five forward Beckham Wyrick from the left wing
wide open for a 3. Bacon 5–2.

Little Dru from the left corner for a 3. High and lofty. His patented
shot. Stays up there forever. Comes back down. 5–5.

Rebound at the other end by Romeo. Over to me. Pull up for a 3
in front of the rim off his screen. St. V 8–5.

Bacon's Hausfeld strong to the glass again. 8–7.

Bacon's six-eight Monty St. Clair is fouled and hits both. 9–8
Bacon.

Third lead change less than 5 minutes in.

Wyrick, boxing me in on the last foul shot, hits me with a forearm. He's a little bit crazy to begin with, more than just aggressive. He's talking trash, letting me know that it's not going to be another St. V rout. He's setting a tone here, and I suddenly realize there is a game to be played. And Wyrick isn't afraid of me: He's good. But he's human.

Coach Dru is dressed in black and white. Nervous and intense. He too knows he has a ball game on his hands. We all do at this point. Bacon moving the ball around well on offense. Crisp and with authority. Strong collapsing defense making it hard for us to puncture the perimeter and get clean shots. And our press isn't working.

Romeo goes inside from the top of the key but misses. Fouled. Shoots two. Makes both. St. V 10–9.

Fourth lead change.

Bacon's Wyrick on a one-hander on a clear path to the hoop. Bacon 11–10.

Fifth lead change.

It is abundantly clear to me they are not intimidated:

I have guys around me that shouldn't be going around me and scoring on me. And I'm unable to dominate on the offensive end. Or the defensive end. I'm not rebounding like I've been able to do.

St. Clair off an offensive rebound. Bacon 13–10.

Romeo on a layup, 13–12.

Romeo again underneath. St. V 14–13.

Sixth lead change.

Bacon's Frank Phillips finishes to the hoop. Bacon 15–14.
Seventh lead change.
Uncharacteristically, Sian senses an odd feeling:

> *We aren't adjusting well to the way the referees are calling*
> *the game, and at the same time we are playing a little timid.*
> *Rebounding is lacking. They are big inside and they are just*
> *outplaying us.*

I pull up for a 3 just outside the line from the right corner.
Eighth lead change.
First period ends.
St. V 17
Roger Bacon 15

SECOND PERIOD BEGINS.

Bacon's ball on turnover. Guard David Johnson on a fast-break layup. Tied 17–17.

Mraz 3-pointer from left corner. St. V 20–17.

Hausfeld open jumper from fifteen feet. Bacon closes to one. St. V 20–19.

Romeo answers with a nice ten-footer from the baseline. A little breathing room now. St. V back up by 3. St. V 22–19.

Bacon's Phillips all alone underneath for a layup. St. V 22–21.

Forget the breathing room.

Romeo makes a crosscourt pass to me. Over to Little Dru in front of the rim for a 3-pointer. Swish. Definitely some breathing room now. St. V 25–21. But Little Dru still feels uncomfortable:

> *We aren't disciplined. We are lazy on defense. We are going for a lot of steals. We don't get them and they take advantage of it, they are scoring on us. We aren't bad on offense, but like I say we aren't disciplined. We always have a tendency to feel the refs are against us, but this game we really let it get to us. I think that has a lot to do with Roger Bacon having control of the game so much.*

St. Clair right back for a turnaround spinner at baseline. Beautiful move. Gap closed to 2. 25–23.

Back and forth. Back and forth. Up and down. Up and down. St. V 27–23. St. V 27–24. Less than 2 minutes left in the first half. Long 3-pointer by Hausfeld. A tie, 27–27.

Fourth tie of the game.

Pick and roll from me to Romeo underneath, off Bacon turnover. St. V 29–27.

Bacon's Phillips moves to the hoop with a left-hander: 29–29.

Fifth tie of game.

Mraz fouled going into the lane. Makes one of two. St. V 30–29.

Bacon turnover with 50 seconds left. Mraz takes a 3-pointer. Misses.

Bacon's Leonard Bush inside with 21 seconds left. Good.

Ninth lead change.

Now I truly am getting jittery:

It just seems like everything is going wrong. Like the wheels are just falling off. Things are happening that never happened before. People are trying to do it by themselves. The referees are calling things that don't seem right. Like everyone has it out for us. It's our fault but we are blaming everyone else. I know that.

Second period ends.
Roger Bacon 31
St. V 30

During halftime, there is a creeping sense of disbelief in the locker room. We are only down by 1, but Roger Bacon is playing with relentlessness and confidence. We silently begin to ask ourselves the same question: Why are we where we are? But I'm beginning to loosen up a little bit now. Going into the second half, Coach Dru is just going to play me in the post; he says, "Hey, they can't stop you in the post."

Third period begins.

I go through the lane off a feed from Little Dru. St. V 32–31.
Tenth lead change.
Bacon's Wyrick returns with a dunk off a lob pass. Bacon 33–32.
Eleventh lead change.
Coach Dru squatting in front of the bench, more unsmiling than ever, motioning the team on. Turnovers traded. Romeo off my feed. St. V 34–33.

Twelfth lead change.

Hausfeld drives to the basket. Bacon 35–34.

Thirteenth lead change.

Romeo puts in a rebound of his own shot, battling off the glass. St. V 36–35. Plus he is fouled. Good. St. V 37–35.

Fourteenth lead change.

Sian decides it's all about destiny:

> We still feel that we are going to win. We have been in situations like this before. We always feel that we are going to pull it out at the end.

Three-pointer by Hausfeld from the left side. Good. Bacon 38–37.

Fifteenth lead change.

Then Bacon on a run. 40–37. 42–37. 44–37. 46–37. 48–37.

I spin into the lane. Gap closed to 48–39.

Another basket off a lob from Little Dru. Bacon 48–41.

Foul shot by Bacon's Phillips. Bacon 49–41.

I answer back with another basket off a feed from Romeo. Bacon 49–43.

Wyrick returns with a baseline jumper with 8 seconds left. Bacon 51–43.

In desperation, I take a running 3-pointer ten feet inside the half-court line. Bank it in as the buzzer sounds.

Third period ends.

Roger Bacon 51

St. V 46

FOURTH PERIOD BEGINS.

Bacon scores on two quick layups. Their lead climbs back up to 9 points. Bacon 55–46. Sian flip-flops back to a sinking feeling:

> *It's almost like a nightmare. You can almost feel people look-*
> *ing at you like, How can you let it slip away? You're sup-*
> *posed to win four straight state championships.*

Coach Dru can feel that pressure building on us, the attitude that we are supposed to win. He feels the weight of those expectations crashing down on us as seventeen-year-olds. He can literally see it.

I score in traffic on a short bank off the glass. Bacon 55–48.

Bacon's Hausfeld answers with his eighteenth and nineteenth point on a ten-footer. Bacon 57–48. Sian is aware of the implications:

> *We are trying to get things on the right road, but they keep*
> *making play after play. And then the crowd turns on us,*
> *starts cheering for them, and that makes things even more*
> *difficult.*

But Romeo answers with his eighteenth and nineteenth point off an offensive rebound, twisting and turning with a strong move inside. And is fouled. Bacon 57–50.

Misses, but teammate Sekou Lewis makes a putback. Bacon 57–52.

Romeo rebounds at the other end. Feeds to Little Dru. Little Dru back to Romeo. Romeo to Mraz. Mraz lobs a pass to me. In close off the glass. Bacon 57–54.

4:40 left.

Romeo is open underneath. I lead him by a hair too much, and the ball skips off his fingers. Out of bounds. Still Bacon 57–54.

Romeo is called for his fourth foul for a reacharound on St. Clair. Makes both ends of a one-and-one. 59–54 Bacon. Romeo knows that one more foul, and he is out of the game. Now he is worried like the rest of us:

> *LeBron's back is ailing him. I'm in foul trouble. Little Dru isn't making his shots. It's just like everything is happening wrong to us at the right time for Roger Bacon. We play them ten times, we beat them in nine.*

3:50 left.

I steal. Dunk. Close the gap to 59–56 Bacon. It isn't over yet.

Bacon upcourt. Romeo blocks from behind on Wyrick. Called for his fifth foul. Out of the game with 2:45 left. Marches to the bench emotional and upset, clenching his uniform shirt in his teeth, his head angled upward searching for explanation. Little Dru can feel the tension mounting ever higher:

> *It definitely hurts when Romeo fouls out of the game. He is playing well. He is in double digits and Roger Bacon has a lot of size and we need him out there. He is in foul trouble for most of the game. Instead of moving on and collecting ourselves and being calm about it, we are still complaining about the refs as much as he is.*

Wyrick makes one of two free throws. 60–56 Bacon.

I weave in traffic to the basket. Off the glass. 60–58 Bacon.

2:12 left.

I dish off to Mraz for a 3-pointer. He misses. Ball back to Bacon. Still 60–58 Bacon.

Sian quickly fouls. St. Clair at the line. Makes first. Misses second. 61–58 Bacon.

1:54 left.

Wyrick slaps it back, so Bacon retains possession. Another quick foul by Sian.

Hausfeld makes first. 62–58 Bacon. Makes second. 63–58.

I go baseline and finish off with a dunk. 63–60 Bacon.

Under a minute left.

Wyrick can't finish on a layup for Bacon. Ball back to St. V.

Little Dru turns it over. He goes for a layup and has the ball flicked out of his hands from behind.

Ball to Phillips. Kisses it off the glass. 65–60 Bacon.

Forty seconds left.

I answer with a 3-point play to give me 32 points for the game. 65–63 Bacon.

Thirty seconds left.

Bacon's Johnson fouled by Little Dru. Misses first. Makes second. 66–63 Bacon.

Twenty-two-point-five seconds left.

Ball inbounded by St. V.

Less than 17 seconds left.

Coach Dru calls time-out. He knows that I'm going to be taken out of the flow by Roger Bacon's defense to prevent me from getting off a good shot. He draws up a play that has Little Dru taking it, and Chad Mraz, typical of their rivalry, is incredulous. "LeBron has brought us all the way back, and you're going to give Little Dru the final shot?" Coach Dru knows his son, convinced it is a comment that Little Dru cannot let go of as he heads back out on the floor.

I dish it off to Mraz. He has hit big shots before, including a crucial 3-pointer as a sophomore to help beat Villa Angela–St. Joseph in the regional championship. He takes the shot here. Open from the left wing for a 3. He misses. Still 66–63 Bacon. But there still is a glimmer.

Hausfeld gets rebound and is fouled from behind. Play is stopped.

Little Dru suddenly takes the ball and hurls it at the rim in frustration. Technical is called on Little Dru. I go up to him and shake him and point to the scoreboard and say, "What are you doing? There's still time left." Little Dru knows exactly what he has just done:

> There is no need to do that right there. It is a blow to our team that really kills us at that moment. They have a chance to seal the deal, but with me making that play, I seal the deal for us.

Unless Roger Bacon misses.

Hausfeld goes to the line. Makes first. Misses second. 67–63 Bacon.

Now the two-shot technical. Makes first. 68–63 Bacon. Makes second. 69–63.

Eight-point-nine seconds left.

And Bacon retains possession because of the technical.

WE ARE NOW HELPLESS. And we are about to accomplish something that seemed unimaginable before the game, no matter how strong the karma. We are about to lose the state championship.

III.

Willie cried after the game. He cried out of embarrassment because he had only gotten in for several minutes and had not helped the team like he felt he should have. He also cried because the goal of winning four state championships in a row had now been shattered. Little Dru covered his eyes with a headband so no one could see his tears. He had not played well, shooting only 2 for 5, and he felt humiliated. He knew that as our General, he had sent us terribly off course with that technical when we were still only down by 3. His fire and brimstone, usually so effective, had gotten the better of him at a pivotal moment. He wasn't pleased with the shot that had been taken right before he hurled the ball at the rim, and he let it show. Romeo had started crying even before the final buzzer, so frustrated by fouling out. When the Roger Bacon team raised the gleaming championship trophy in joyous victory on the parquet floor of the Value City Arena, rising ten stories high, Romeo reverted back to the old ways that he had tried to correct somewhat. He wanted to fight. He wanted to punch somebody. Then he realized there was nothing he could do about it. It was out of St. V's hands now. Roger Bacon had won through balance and outrebounding and greater team discipline. Four of its players were in double digits. The rebounding difference was 32 to 18. Of the 63 points we had scored, Romeo and I had accounted for 51.

Little Dru tried to walk immediately into the locker room, but his father ran and brought him back out into the arena to be gracious in defeat. But he was inconsolable. Sian had his arms around Little Dru, rocking him back and forth, cradling him and trying to calm him down like a gentle father to a son. "Just be strong and don't worry, you know we'll be back," he told Little Dru "And when we come back, we'll be stronger than ever."

Sian refused to wear the silver medallion given out for finishing second. On the inside he was stoic, because he knew what had gone down and why it had gone down; we deserved to lose, not only because of how we'd played against Roger Bacon but because of how we'd treated the entire season. We *had* fooled around too much. We *had* clashed with Coach Dru too much. We *had* ignored his dire predictions that our actions on and off the court would ultimately be fatal.

We were still also teenage kids, with no idea how to handle our sudden fame. The media, *Sports Illustrated* first and foremost, had lit a bonfire under us, and then watched the inevitable immolation. The magazine had supposedly carefully considered the decision to put a high school junior on the cover, but I believe they must have known the explosion it would cause. No one in high school deserves to be compared to Michael Jordan, and no one in high school could be expected to withstand the pressure of such a comparison. We had become bigheaded jerks, I in particular, and we are to blame for that, but so are adults who treated us that way and then sat back and smugly watched the self-destruction.

As Sian stood in the arena, he was struck by how happy so many fans were that we'd lost. He heard them chattering back and forth: "I told you so. I told you they weren't that good." As an assistant coach, his father, Lee, had obviously wanted to win the game, but mostly he had just wanted the year to come to an end. The emotion he felt the most was relief. The season of agony was finally over.

In the locker room there was almost complete silence, except for the sound of Romeo flushing his silver medallion down the toilet. When Coach Dru spoke, his main concern was getting the players to understand that all was not lost. Little Dru had taken it hard. Romeo had taken it hard. Willie had taken it hard. More than just losing, Coach Dru was concerned about our mental well-being. But he went home and didn't sleep that night, poring over and over in his mind what he could have done differently. The game had been called tightly by the refs, too tightly, as far as he was concerned. That was part of the game of basketball, however, and you learned to adapt to it. Here the calls had so clearly upset us as players, crawled into our heads. In the huddle during breaks, instead of talking about the way we were playing and what we needed to do, we had constantly complained about the refereeing. As he relived the game, Coach Dru, being the kind of man he was, once again assumed full responsibility for not taking control on the sidelines to reel us back in. He refused to place the blame on anyone else, when the truth was, we deserved the vast bulk of it.

As dignified as he was in defeat, the loss in the state championship was his worst scenario, what had haunted him from the beginning when he mulled over whether to take the head coaching job in the first place: If I win, it's because I had Keith Dambrot's kids. If I lose, it's my fault. He had to contend with Little Dru's technical at the end; given the intensity of their relationship, that wasn't so easy either. Then came a column in the *Akron Beacon Journal* stating the very thing he had feared people would conclude about why St. V had not won its third straight state championship: "The biggest difference between this year's St. V–M team and the past two is the leader—Dru Joyce." He read the column at the kitchen counter early in the morning. Little Dru read it next, then Carolyn. Coach Dru's first impulse was to send an angry letter. The point of it would be not simply to defend himself, but to ask the writer how he could say such things after all that Coach Dru had done for kids in basketball over the years. But Little Dru said to his father: "Dad, don't worry about it. We're going to show them next season." There are times when words of clarity come from unexpected places, and this was one of those times; his son's comment pulled Coach Dru back to reality, rather than let him go off on a tangent that would lead nowhere. Carolyn Joyce chimed in:

"Dru's right. Let's just show people who you guys really are." Coach Dru dropped the idea of the letter, because he knew his son and his wife were right.

He also played over in his mind a quote from Roger Bacon's coach, Bill Brewer, who said, "We knew they had the best player—we thought we had the best team." Just as he had overcome the column, he resolved in his mind that no one, no one, would ever say that again about a squad he coached.

As for me, I felt remarkably calm in defeat, the karma of the morning being all I needed to know that it had ended up the way I was afraid it would. I was comfortable with what I had done in the final moments on the court because that's what I had done the whole year and would continue to do throughout my career—look for the open man—and Mraz was open, and he was a good 3-point shooter. If Little

Dru was upset, so be it. I shed no tears, blamed no one except all of us. I went down the row of Roger Bacon players, shook each of their hands because they had earned their victory. Something else happened then and there: I knew that things would have to change, everything would have to change senior year, if the Fab Four Plus One was ever going to achieve the dream of winning a national championship. Because there was a harsh truth:

Time was running out.

12.

In or Out?

I.

One of the first orders of business was Romeo. His temperament had improved over the two years he had been at St. V. He had learned the need for outside opinions. As hard as it was, he had learned to be slightly more open, because we as the Fab Four expected that. But still, too often, he acted against the world, against everything. We didn't like it. We didn't like the idea of the Fab Four Plus One. We wanted Romeo to be with us. But he didn't make it easy. His ability to offend was still there. So were his trust issues.

With only one year left, we had to do something. We couldn't go on like this with Willie and Little Dru and Sian and me inside and Romeo outside. We had now known Romeo since we were sophomores. We knew that he liked to be with us, just as we liked to be with him. We also knew that he still liked to play the role of the tough guy who didn't need to rely on anyone else, with his frequent rejoinders of "I don't care" or "fuck you." We knew that he still liked being a contrarian, the kind of person who, if a dinner was planned for 7:00 p.m., would immediately insist that he wasn't going until 8:00 p.m. It wasn't good for our heads. It wasn't good for his head. And it wasn't good for our team. Romeo himself realized he had to do something. That tough guy act, the "screw you I don't need anybody" attitude, was no longer working for him, wearing thin. There wasn't any payoff in the badass image he had cultivated, and he wanted to connect with the Fab Four. "I felt he was crying out for something," said his sister De Shawnda. We drew such sustenance from one another, and Romeo wanted that same sustenance but could not seem to get there. Much of it, perhaps, had come from changing schools. He had lost many friends, a percentage of them who still felt he was a pimp for going to a Catholic school that was over 85 percent white. The feelings of alienation also traced back to the abandonment of the past. "It caused him to get angry and develop a resistance toward people because he had gotten hurt," said De Shawnda, who was four years older. "He became a tough guy even though he had never gotten into a real fight in his life. He overcame pain by being negative." But Romeo finally saw that it wasn't worth it to have people dislike him and look at him and say to themselves, He's an asshole. He was living with his grandmother, and much like Little Dru, she saw behind the curtain. She saw a Romeo who could be incredibly kind when he felt like it, willing to give the shirt off his back to someone who was in need.

We took an informal vote in the school cafeteria on whether or not to embrace Romeo, expand the Fab Four, and literally rename it so that everybody would know we were the Fab Five. We agreed, as Little Dru had once put it, that Romeo was blowing smoke most of the time, and that the best way to handle it was by calling his bluff. We knew that he was always going to have moments of wig-out, and that you just had to accept it and move on. But underneath was a Romeo who had matured.

Little Dru, despite their initial differences, articulated it best that day: "This is a guy that we can trust. And that's what you look for in a friend." As for basketball, there had been a complete turnaround. When Romeo first started playing at Central-Hower, "I didn't give a shit," as he later put it. He saw that the seniors had all kinds of girls and all kinds of clothes, and he wanted in on that. But as he began to work harder at St. V, he fell in love with the game, felt crippled without it.

When we told him that the Fab Four would now be known as the Fab Five, he tried to act like it didn't mean anything to him. He said, "Thanks guys," with a corny look on his face. Whatever the reaction, you could tell he was excited. To Romeo, it meant that the Fab Four wasn't arrogant, but a group of individuals who enjoyed being around one another and lived for each other. It was important to him to become part of the group; no matter what self-image you project, you still want to be part of something. He fully opened up to us, talked about what he had been through as a child, where the selfishness and self-protectiveness had come from. He was initially uncomfortable with the affection we gave each other, but he even got over that. "I felt this was the turning point in his life," said De Shawnda.

He also found great inspiration in how Willie handled the news that he wouldn't be a regular starter senior year, but a role player off the bench. Basketball had just become star-crossed for Willie after the shoulder separation surgery. It put him behind the rest of us, and he could never quite catch up. He became nervous about reinjuring his shoulder. He could never get fully in shape. He simply lost his touch, and it was sad to witness. Sometimes his frustration became almost unbearable, given how good he had been in junior high. His body had disappointed him even further by failing to grow to six-seven, as many had predicted it would. As a senior, he was about the same height as he had been in eighth grade, six-two.

In junior year, Willie played what he considered to be the worst game of his life—turning it over, fouling a player on a 3-point shot. He felt like he was hurting the team; maybe even more difficult, he no longer felt comfortable on the basketball court. He dressed quickly afterward and hurried to the team bus before the rest of us. Sitting alone on the bus, he began to cry. He'd pulled himself together by the time the rest of us appeared, but I could tell something was wrong. "Are you all right?" I asked him. He said he was, but I knew he was bleeding inside. He couldn't help but hearken back to junior high school and ask himself the wrenching question: What had happened?

It was hard for him to see the rest of us thriving on the court while he struggled. It was hard to him to see most of us getting recruiting letters for college for either basketball or football when he was not. But Willie was also expanding, to the degree that basketball did not dominate his life as it once had. He was making great strides in football after he switched positions from receiver to quarterback: he had a splendid arm, although there was always some question as to where the ball was going to land. It was also important to Willie that he be seen by other students at St. V as not just an athlete. He had been on the student council in junior high school, and he decided he wanted to do something similar at St. V. He also wanted to deflect the negative feelings that some students had about us. So he decided to run for junior class president and started preparing a speech. When he gave it in the cafeteria, Sian and Romeo and Little Dru and I sat in the front row and somehow stifled the urge to tease him a little bit. He didn't look at us, because he knew he would crack up. Willie was sincere about why this office mattered to him and what he could do for the school. He said he didn't simply want to be considered a jock. He suggested such ideas as a talent show, a 1970s-themed dance, and a sleep-in in the gym for the junior and senior classes. The four of us got to our feet afterward and gave him a standing ovation, and teachers, almost surprised by Willie's heartfelt words, were impressed.

When it came time to vote, Willie was pretty sure that Sian and Romeo and Little Dru and I voted more than once, since more ballots were cast than there were students in the junior class (I have "no comment"). That's "love," as Willie later put it, and he said he would have done the same had one of us been running for class president. There was controversy, but Willie was ultimately named the winner, the first African American at St. V since the 1970s to be elected president of a class.

He helped organize the junior prom and the junior-senior prom. He made sure that fund-raisers like the bake sale ran smoothly, and he represented the class to the board of the school on certain issues. He did also help to humanize the basketball team in the eyes of our classmates. He let other students know that we did want to be part of school life at St. V beyond what we did on the parquet floor.

A lesser person than Willie would have quit basketball, or

transferred to a school where he'd get more playing time, as some were urging him to do. Neither of those options were true to Willie's character. He still wanted to contribute, whatever that contribution might be, and he would not abandon his brothers.

He knew he'd been depressed junior year, and he was determined to be a different kind of player senior year, to accept whatever Coach Dru had in mind for him, then do his very best with it. Romeo was deeply affected by Willie's selflessness. In fact, Willie's example had a huge influence on Romeo. If Willie could set aside his disappointments and adapt himself to the team's needs, Romeo believed that maybe he could too. He also admired Willie's maturity. When Coach Dru told us to get some sleep because we had a game the next day, even though we weren't tired, it was Willie who would say, "You need to go to sleep so you can be more prepared for the game." When a player got silly on the court, Willie would get straight in his face and say, "You're wrong. Stop it."

When Romeo became one of the Fab Five, the bond between us only grew stronger. We were with each other from 8:00 a.m., when school started, to 8:00 p.m., when practice ended. Afterward we usually stayed at each other's houses and apartments. I always wanted companionship, so when other members of the Fab Five came over to my apartment, I tried to basically kidnap them for days. A tradition continued that a booster would bring us several large pizzas after a game, usually followed by a trip to Swensons, where Little Dru once did the eating equivalent of going for the cycle by ordering a double cheeseburger, a milk shake, fries, and a Coney dog, only to be denied by the Coney dog.

From the very start, senior year was different. We had all sifted through the events of junior year; we had all realized how our heads had gotten the better of us. We all thought about the loss to Roger Bacon, which still stung and humiliated us. We all looked for ways we could change, improve, focus. We vowed to stop fooling around academically. "Everybody was planning on going to college, so it was a must now," said Sian, whose antics junior year had made him academically ineligible for the first five games of the football season senior year. "It was getting late in the game, so you couldn't be messing around and messing your grades up." A rule was instituted in the locker room where we could no longer listen to music out loud.

Coach Dru had also heard rumors junior year that the Fab Four Plus One had gotten access to a hotel room in the Akron area, invited girls over, and either drank or smoked marijuana. He called us into his office, with those walls as pale as the fog of an early morning.

He started first with Willie, because he knew Willie could never lie.

"Willie, man, I'm hearing some crazy stuff. What's going on? I'm hearing you guys are getting high, trying to put a towel under the door at the hotel thinking that the smell isn't going outside. Acting foolish."

He looked at Willie, and Coach Dru knew all he needed to know. "So it is true."

Willie admitted that he had been smoking marijuana in the hotel room, and it was true that he wasn't the only one who had been misbehaving. Little Dru, Sian, and I had smoked as well, and Romeo had been drinking.

He looked over at his son.

"I've been honest with you. I told you what drugs have done, how it ruined my early life and my early opportunities in sports."

Coach Dru was never going to be a great athlete, but he had lost his direction when he began to party. That's why he had gone to Ohio University—it was known as a party school—and it wasn't about sports anymore. He mainly smoked marijuana, but he experimented with all kinds of other drugs. He recognized a few years later that he had lost his direction without sports, and without sports, he almost went off the deep end.

"My life has been an open book to you," he said to his son. "I haven't hidden that from you."

Coach Dru could just imagine the publicity.

"What kind of nonsense is this? Can you imagine the headlines tomorrow? St. V starting five arrested in a hotel. Possession of marijuana. You guys have to be smarter than that."

Coach Dru also realized we were still typical teenagers. But he wanted to put an end to such activity for the rest of our high school days at St. V, not only as juniors but also as seniors. From that point forward such carrying-on did end, although Sian was defiant.

"I'm going to keep smoking."

"Sian, you're making a big mistake."

Later on, the repercussions of this stance would help ruin an opportunity unlike any other.

I ALSO HAD TO MAKE a decision about football senior year. I loved football. The last thing I wanted to do was give it up. It was wrenching to think I might not play. Some smart people, including my mother, told me I was crazy to run the risk of an injury, forfeit the increasing possibility of a professional career in basketball. I had already broken the index finger on my nonshooting hand. But I played football anyway for three years. No matter where my skills were taking me, I did not want my persona at St. V to be defined solely as "LeBron James, basketball player." Plus, part of high school is doing what you love. I have to say, I wasn't half bad at it. As a wide receiver on the St. V team that went 10 and 4 junior year and made the playoffs, I gained 1,310 yards on 52 receptions and caught 15 touchdown passes and was all-state in our division. Some scouting lists rated me as the number-one receiver in the country. Sadly I walked away from football senior year; I would dedicate myself fully to basketball.

Coach Dru rededicated himself as well, after a period of soul-searching in which he weighed whether we were too old—or he was too soft—for him to lead us effectively. In the end, he heeded the advice his son and wife had given him at the kitchen counter. He had been a little bit too tentative junior year, trying to please everyone. Now he showed a newfound decisiveness. He talked with Coach Culp, who he felt had spent the previous season trying to undermine him at times and remembers saying, "You have a choice—either you support me and support the team, or you leave." Coach Culp doesn't recall receiving such an ultimatum. He does recollect Coach Dru telling him that they had to be "on the same page" together, and he stayed on as an assistant.

He listened this time to the coach at the Kent State clinic who had said that one of the first things a new head coach must do is confront the parents. The meeting took place at the school library several weeks before the season. Knowing he could not go through another year like the one before, he bluntly laid out the conditions of discussion: "I will be happy to talk about ways in which your sons can improve their games. But there are three areas in which this conversation immediately ends—playing time, strategy, or another player."

The most significant gathering of the season, though, was a team meeting in the locker room before the first practice. It was decorated with a padded floor of gold carpet with the words *Fighting Irish* imprinted on it. On one wall was a green leprechaun stretching his fist in defiance. On another wall was a plastic board that Coach Dru had put up, bearing the following words in green: *Humility, Unity, Discipline, Thankfulness, Servanthood, Integrity,* and *Passion.* There were thirty-three lockers in the room, all of them painted dark green. The looks on our faces were somber and serious, no time for jokes and backslapping. We had done enough of that. The locker room had been remodeled, and I sat at my locker, number 29. Little Dru was at number 22. Romeo was at number 17. Sian was at number 20, and Willie was at number 21. We were there by ourselves without any coaches, and then Willie spoke: "This is our last year together. If anybody says anything about Coach Dru, I'm going at them. I won't have it." As for me, I knew at that moment I would have to step up and become a leader, and my words were succinct: "Let's just go ahead and take care of business and win a national championship."

We were angry. We were ashamed of the year before. We were inspired by *USA Today*'s preseason national rankings, which placed St. V twenty-third in the nation. We viewed that as a slap—and a spur. We were better than that. Now we had to prove it.

In the effort to fulfill the dream and win the national championship, St. V had a schedule worthy of a Division I college team, with trips to Los Angeles, New Jersey, North Carolina, Philadelphia, and Pittsburgh to compete against other top-ranked high schools. Some called the travel excessive, but there was no other way—the caliber of your competition was a key component in how you were ranked.

Back home, games had already been moved to the University of Akron because of its seating capacity. St. V could now charge $12 a ticket for an assigned seat, netting nearly half a million dollars from the Fab Five the last two years we played. A northern Ohio cable company put ten of our contests on pay-per-view at $7.95 a game. Our game at the Palestra in Philadelphia would draw a sell-out crowd of 8,722, and over 200 media credentials would be issued even though the fabled arena had only 87 press seats. Our game at Pauley Pavilion in Los Angeles would draw another sell-out crowd, this one 12,500 strong. Our game at the Greensboro Coliseum would draw more than 15,000, the largest in the basketball-mad high school history of North Carolina. Our game at the Sovereign Bank Arena in Trenton would draw 8,600—yet another sell-out.

Despite all the travel, we never missed a day of school. When we left town, we played either on weekends or on holidays. Was it insane for a high school basketball team to jet around the country? At the time I thought it was exciting, going to places I never ever thought I would get to see in my life when I was a scared, lonely young boy. Now I believe it was excessive. I believe it was too much, for us and every other high school around the country that followed a schedule similar to ours. So I applaud the rule since passed by the Ohio High

School Athletic Association essentially banning travel of more than three hundred miles in any one direction. I can virtually guarantee that when we traveled, there were plenty of promoters who enjoyed a nice payday off of us as high school kids, knowing that our presence would fill arenas.

The media hype that had surrounded us junior year would only multiply senior year. There would be more autographs. More followers. More reporters, to the degree that Coach Dru closed practices not only to outsiders but to the media. More girls begging to know where we were staying when we played in North Carolina and, Sian, being Sian, yelling out the name of the hotel, so the lobby was packed when we got there. One woman hopped on the team bus and took her shirt off. Two autograph seekers drove two hours from New York to Philadelphia and waited outside the Doubletree Hotel for hours until the team bus arrived just so they could get my autograph. I guess I should have felt flattered, but instead I thought, These guys need to get a life, and I'm not it. A meaningless preseason scrimmage in nearby Brunswick, Ohio, attracted 950 people, the watchful presence of police, and four television stations and three newspapers.

The *Late Show with David Letterman* and *The Oprah Winfrey Show* called and invited me to appear. *Live with Regis and Kelly* called to see if I would shoot baskets with Regis Philbin himself (I'm pretty sure I could have taken him). One mother called to see if I would attend her son's bar mitzvah. A steady stream of men came into the school claiming to be my father. Some of the celebrity was flattering. Some of it was funny. But some of it was also growing darker and darker, as more people simply hoped I would fail, the whole point of the media to build me up to absurd proportions no matter what my age so they then could beat me down. It was early in my life to learn such a lesson, but I learned it.

When we held that team meeting, we had only a vague idea of the roadblocks and distractions that lay in front of us. But we already had a sense it would not be easy. To remind ourselves, before each practice we touched the words that Coach Dru had put up on the wall. If you weren't willing to abide by them, Sian said, "Don't come out."

WE OPENED THE SEASON against Wellston High School in the gym at St. V. It was a rare opportunity to truly play at home, and the place was packed. We wanted two games at the St. V gym while school officials would have liked all of them at the Rhodes Arena because of the revenue it generated. Coach Dru took the issue to the board of the school, arguing that we really weren't getting the high school experience we deserved since we regarded the Rhodes Arena as a neutral court. The board granted the request, but as usual there was an added degree of hoopla: in addition to playing at St. V, it was also our first game televised on cable. In keeping with the take-no-prisoners approach we had promised one another, we led 23–2 at the end of the first quarter, then stretched the lead to 45–10 with about a minute left before halftime. Romeo led all scorers with 15 when he went to the line for a free-throw attempt. The ball went up; the lights went out. Officials had to cancel the game on account of a power failure. Other parts of Akron lost power as well, the rumor rife that the outage had been caused by an overload of wires snaking in every which direction at the St. V gym, which simply wasn't equipped to handle a live cable event.

As a believer in karma, I wasn't sure what to think, except that it was just a weird way to begin the season, up by 35 and not even getting the win because it was too dark to see. (For all I know, Romeo's free throw is still floating up there.) If nothing else, that shortened first game did foreshadow the rhythm of the season. Stuff *was* going to happen.

The first full game of the season, against George Junior Republic, also had a special flavor. Coach Dru remembered the way they had played the previous year, with those hard fouls all over the place and knocking me to the floor. Before this game, he heard an assistant coach for George Junior talk to his players in a way that Coach Dru thought was encouraging them to play dirty once again. For the first and only time in his career, Coach Dru decided to bury another team. The final score was 101 to 40, and he had the team pressing until the very last second.

"You have no class," the George Junior coach said afterward.

"I don't care," Coach Dru responded.

In a postgame press conference, Coach Dru addressed the issue of dirty play after it had been brought up by a reporter. When he was getting on the team bus, the assistant coach stepped off his own bus.

"I understand you didn't like what I had to say to my players. I can say whatever I want."

"It sounds like you were inciting them to play dirty."

The assistant coach then challenged Coach Dru to a fight.

"If you got a problem, we can settle it right here."

Coach Dru just laughed and walked away, although running up the score like that was something he later deeply regretted.

The near-brawl didn't distract us from what was looming on our horizon. In the third game of the season awaited an opponent that would make our dream or destroy it. We would face our old foe, whom we had never beaten, whom we had to beat now.

Oak Hill.

Oak Hill ranked number one in the country—undefeated at 7 and 0. The game would be broadcast live on ESPN2, with Bill Walton and Dick Vitale and Dan Shulman doing the commentary. As usual, Oak Hill boasted a host of Division I signees on their way to schools like Virginia and Connecticut and Ohio State. We would meet them at the Convocation Center at Cleveland State University, which basically gave us home-court advantage. But how much of a difference would that really make against Oak Hill?

II.

It doesn't look promising in the first quarter. We're playing too tight. Missed jumpers. Fadeaways falling short. Turnovers. Oak Hill is by no means perfect, but they're methodical, patient. Before we know it, we are down 13–5 after Isaiah Swann hits a 3-pointer for Oak Hill. They are playing with poise, and we're not. It's as simple as that. We are clearly nervous, not doing what we know we can do. We need to collect ourselves, breathe a little bit, forget about Dick Vitale and Bill Walton. Forget about the more than a hundred reporters attending the game. Forget about the pro scouts who have come to watch.

It's still 13–5, with less than 2 minutes left in the period. Coach

Dru calls a time-out: "It's time for us to get going. It's early, but you don't want to get blown out in your hometown on national television, so you guys better wake up."

Oak Hill commits a turnover. I score on a dunk off a feed from Brandon Weems to make it 13–7. Weems follows with a 3-pointer. The gap is closed to 13–10. Oak Hill is called for a 3-second violation; their poise is beginning to wear off a bit.

We inbound and take the ball upcourt. Over to Sian. Sian over to me on a perfect feed. I maneuver over Swann for a layup inside to make the score 13–12. The first period comes to a close, and we are back in the thick of it.

At least we think we are, until consecutive 3-pointers by Maurice Williams and J. R. Reynolds stretch Oak Hill's lead to 7 at the start of the second period. Collect. Take a breath. Collect. Take a breath. That mantra must guide how we play if we are going to win. No panic. No fear. No panic. No fear. That's another mantra we must keep reciting to ourselves. I get a lob pass from Sian and score on a layup off the glass. 19–14. Then a two-handed dunk off an Oak Hill turnover. 19–16. Then Romeo, who is just beginning to get into the flow of the game, steals the ball and is fouled trying to make a layup. He hits both free throws. 19–18.

We continue the burst of momentum. No panic. No fear. No panic. No fear. Romeo makes a 3-point play to give us the lead for the first time, 21–19. We stretch that lead to 5 by the end of the first half, 30–25.

Oak Hill is Oak Hill. We know that. So do they. It's why they have a record of 155 and 4 the past five seasons.

With 2:54 left in the third period, they regain the lead by 1, 41–40, when Ivan Harris, on his way to Ohio State, hits a jumper in between two defenders. Is this the moment where we fold and fade away? Is this the moment where, so early in the season, the dream just dies?

Sian is wide open for a fifteen-footer with 2:18 left in the period. The ball tickles the rim, plays with it, taunts it, and then finally plops in. It gives us back the lead, 42–41. We go up by 7 at the end of the third period, 50–43. Then Willie begins the fourth quarter with a 3-pointer to make it 53–43. We score 6 more unanswered points after that, my favorite play when I bring the ball upcourt, pass it to Little Dru, who passes it to Sian, who takes one dribble toward the basket and then bounce-passes it to Romeo, who lays it in with his left hand. The play is a Fab Five thing of beauty, so in tune it's almost like magic, much like the final score against the nation's top-ranked team:

St. V 65

Oak Hill 45

In the locker room afterward, Romeo, wearing only a pair of shorts and some ankle bracelets, runs around like a little kid, jumping up and down, tackling players. He feels the euphoria of slaying the nemesis, the bully who has been kicking your ass for years until you finally say, "I'm not taking this anymore."

WE MOVED UP TO NINTH in the *USA Today* poll, but we had a way to go to get to the top despite just puncturing the giant. It wasn't impossible: we were still alive, which is all we could ask for at that point. The glow of the victory lasted. At least for several weeks.

III.

Sian agonized. He cried. He went back and forth. He made up his mind. He changed it. He knew what to do. He didn't. Every step of the way he was racked by guilt. Was he turning his back on the Fab Five? Was he turning his back on his brothers?

With his six-three height and his weight approaching 300 pounds, his future lay in football, not basketball. He was tough and he was mean and he had those quick feet, and big-time schools like Miami and Ohio State were seriously looking at him in terms of an athletic scholarship. He had a chance to high-light those skills on the defensive line when he was invited to partici-pate in the U.S. Army All-American Bowl in San Antonio in early January, featuring eighty of the nation's top players. Reggie Bush would be there. Brady Quinn would be there. How could Sian not go?

Because nothing in life is ever as simple as it seems.

If he went to the All-American Bowl, Sian would miss our game against Mater Dei High School in Los Angeles at the Pauley Pavilion. Mater Dei was ranked fourth in the country, and given the way our respective seasons had shaken out, this game could determine whether we or they would rise to number one in the USA Today poll. We had waited what seemed like a lifetime to get to that top spot; now we were in range, having beaten another nationally ranked team, Colum-bus Brookhaven, in overtime, thanks to maybe the greatest karma of all during my four seasons at St. V.

BROOKHAVEN IS RANKED SIXTH. They are coming off a state championship in the highest-ranked division in Ohio, Division I, and they
feel like St. V is getting all the ink when they are the best team in the
state. The game is being played in Columbus at the Value City Arena,
which they feel gives them another distinct advantage as the home
team. Their ace is five-seven All-American point guard Drew Lavender, perhaps the third best at his position in the country; headed for
the University of Oklahoma. With the score tied 59–59 in the final
vapors of the fourth quarter, Lavender strips me of the ball and goes
the other way. It seems like a sure basket and a sure win for Brookhaven.
Lavender has lightning speed, but Sian, rumbling down the court,
somehow catches up with him.

The referee calls an intentional foul, giving Lavender two foul
shots with 2.7 seconds left. Because of the call, nobody guards the line
when Lavender, with 25 points in the game and an 80-percent-plus
free-throw shooter, gets ready. We can only watch across the center
court line with our hands on our hips, our faces glum and covered
with the dull-eyed glaze of resignation, knowing that we are going to
lose. There is no other outcome. Little Dru is losing it inside; he can't
believe this is actually happening, feels like everything is just gone.

Lavender takes the first shot.

It hits the side of the rim and bounces out.

We still stand there helpless to do anything except watch a second
time, figures of loneliness across that center court line, the dream on
a thread that is about to break.

Lavender takes the shot.

It hits off the front of the rim and bounces out.

Now he is the one bowing his head in agony. And the karma is too spectacular to let us down. We outscore Brookhaven 8–3 in the 4-minute overtime to win, 67–62. Still somehow unbeaten.

IF WE BEAT MATER DEI, it would give us a record of 8 and 0. It would also mean that three of those wins had come against teams ranked in the top ten.

Sian too had waited what seemed like a lifetime. Playing without him seemed impossible to contemplate. How could the Fab Five forge ahead, in maybe its biggest and most important game ever, without Sian?

Sian was struggling with the same question. It was a complicated issue, just as Sian himself was complicated. He may have liked playing the role of the bad boy at times. He sported a fake gold tooth for a while as a freshman. He often misplaced things, like his letter jacket. He lost his state championship ring from sophomore year and had to buy a replacement. He knew there had been moments of rebellion junior year when he hadn't listened to anyone. He was well aware of how his poor academic average had cost him dearly, since he was a highly promising football recruit. Of all the members of the Fab Five, he felt most acutely that he wasn't wanted at St. V, did not belong there. At the very least, he felt like he was in no-man's-land. He wondered if the school, particularly as controversy unfolded, enjoyed the success that the Fab Five had brought to St. V, but wanted to go back to the old days and do it primarily with players who had come up through the Catholic Youth Organization. "We brought a lot of good attention," Sian said later. "But they wished we could have been white. They wished every-thing could be the same, but they could do it with white kids." There was also the Block—we liked to congregate there, and Sian resented it when one particular teacher kept telling us to disperse.

Beyond St. V, he keenly felt the racism that sometimes existed when we played away; it burned inside him, while the rest of us were more inclined to just let it go. During one game, fans in the stands repeatedly used the word *nigger*. An opposing player, inbounding the ball after a change of possession, hit Sian in the face with it, an act that he interpreted as racially motivated—which only caused Sian to move in a step closer, fearless as he was.

But beyond his nickname, the Brawl Street Bully, there was a soul-fulness and complexity that went beyond sports. Coach Dru felt that Sian liked to play the role of the thug even though it wasn't his true nature. As a child he had taken tap-dance lessons, and he was a good writer and loved writing poetry (so good that friends paid him to write love poems to girls they liked)—not the qualities you expected to find in someone who fancied himself as Warren Sapp on the football field and Charles Oakley on the basketball court. His dedication to the Fab Five bordered on the religious. At one point he felt we had become more family to him than his own. When we were young, he would make excuses to his parents—like telling them I needed his help on a school project—just so he could stay with me.

At first he decided to just pass on the All-American Bowl. At one point he hoped that the organizers of the football game would let him go to California to be with us at the Pauley Pavilion, then fly back to participate. But they said no, presumably because they didn't want anything to overshadow the game and other activities associated with it. So he would have to make a decision one way or another. And as he sat there crying with his family, not knowing what to do, they pointed out that he had to think about his own future. The All-American Bowl was a showcase. Dozens of college recruiters would be there. The exposure he would get could not be matched by anything else senior year. He knew what he had to do, and we knew it too: he had to play in that football game. There was no other choice, and the Fab Five supported him. He would be missed. There was no doubt about that. We might even lose without him, and knowing Sian, he would never forgive himself if that happened. As brothers, the best thing we could do, the only thing we could do, was reduce his level of guilt as much as possible. Not for a second did we think he was running out on us.

But we still had to compete without him.

EVEN BEFORE THE GAME, the vibe and atmosphere have a nasty scent. A withering story in the *Los Angeles Times* makes us out to be a group of spoiled louts jetting about the country. The story incenses Coach Dru, who crafted the schedule for competitive reasons, and also to give players at the end of the bench the opportunity to be in such famous venues as the Pauley Pavilion and the Palestra. There is the squabble before the game over who should have the UCLA locker room. Coach Dru insists that St. V should be there, and was given such a promise by the promoter; the Mater Dei team, which has been in the UCLA locker room, is moved out. There is even a controversy over what game ball should be used. Since Spalding is the game's sponsor, we have been practicing all week with a Spalding basketball instead of the usual Rawlings one used in Ohio. But Mater Dei is sponsored by Nike, and they keep switching the ball from Spalding to Nike, until a referee steps in and declares Spalding the game ball.

Maybe it's one of the few times, perhaps the only one, where I can't shake the hype out of my head—the stretch limo that picked us up at the airport in Los Angeles (something the promoter of the game, not St. V, arranged and paid for); the scalpers selling tickets for two to three times face value; fans buying merchandise with my face on it, hoping that it might be worth something if I excel in the NBA some-day. Maybe it's playing in Pauley Pavilion, the hallowed home of John Wooden and the UCLA Bruins and their seven consecutive national championships. Maybe it's the fact that ESPN2 is again broadcasting the game live. Maybe it's the sneaker face-off, with Phil Knight and other Nike officials taking up virtually a whole row, and Sonny Vaccaro and the Adidas people in a row of their own. Maybe it's the white uniforms Adidas supplied us, with our names on the back. Maybe it's the room Adidas set up at a hotel, with new sweat suits and new shoes and new towels that read "St. Mary–St. Vincent" and new T-shirts, once again personalized with our names on the back. Maybe it's this. Maybe it's that. Whatever it is, nothing is clicking.

We should be highly motivated. In addition to the number-one ranking on the line, we're seeing this game as payback time. Some of Mater Dei's players may not remember us from eighth grade, but we remember them. We remember them as the backbone of the SoCal All-Stars, the team that beat us by 2 in the finals of the fourteen-and-under AAU tournament. We remember how they treated us like a bunch of hicks until they suddenly had a game on their hands. We remember Travante Nelson and Wesley Washington.

Even with the added incentive, I can't get untracked. I am playing terribly. My jumper is off. I don't have a single 3-pointer. I haven't had any opportunity for dunks on breakaways. Maybe Sian's absence has gotten to me more than I ever thought it would, although Willie has done a nice job of filling the void. After the first period, it's tied at 11–11. In the second period, for the first and only time, I get a little traction going. I hit 5 of 8 shots to help give us a 30–24 lead at halftime (I went 3 for 16 the rest of the night).

It's why I have teammates. Romeo makes a 3-point play in the third quarter. Corey Jones adds two 3-pointers, and we expand the lead to 14 points, 41–27. With the presence of D. J. Strawberry—the son of Darryl Strawberry, and on his way to Maryland—and Wesley Washington, Mater Dei is too strong not to make some kind of run. Washington, who ends up with 18 points for the game, hits a pair of 3-pointers to close the margin to 6 with little more than 4 minutes left. Can he keep it going? Can Mater Dei keep it going?

Time is ticking down. They start fouling to try to get the ball back. Little Dru and Corey Jones combine for six free throws.

We get out of there with a 64–58 victory.

WE HAD BEATEN the fourth-ranked team in the country despite the absence of Sian. We'd won despite playing one of our more lackluster games of the season. That Tuesday, back in Akron, Little Dru went to the library and scanned the sports section of *USA Today* for the high school basketball rankings. We were number one. Now all we had to do was stay there for the rest of the season.

Then all hell broke loose. Again.

13.

Pressure

I.

Maybe the timing could have been better when my mom decided to buy me a Hummer in honor of my birthday. Maybe she should have waited until after the season to avoid the controversy that erupted in the immediate afterglow of our defeat of Mater Dei and our number-one ranking. With the season over, the purchase might have provided less ammunition to the vultures so eager to destroy me and my team. There might have been less at stake, although I don't think the timing mattered one bit. I wasn't just a high school basketball phenom anymore. I was a perpetual target.

I know how the Hummer looked from afar, just as I know how desperate my mom was to do something special for me to honor my eighteenth birthday. I know that the base price of the vehicle, around

$50,000, was far more than our net worth, because we didn't have any net worth. As the national media jumped on top of one another like excited spectators at a car crash, the equally ravenous Ohio High School Athletic Association scrutinized the loan my mom had gotten with the kind of intensity the IRS reserved for a mobster's tax return. I cannot tell you how humiliating it was. Not for me, because I have always been able to screen out what needs to be screened out, but for my mother. After an investigation lasting more than two weeks, the loan did check out; it was legally obtained, and there was no hidden third party behind it trying to win my favor, assuming I went straight to the NBA from high school. Newspaper columnists and television commentators all over the country still continued to have a feast—how could a woman living in a rental-assistance apartment with her son qualify for a loan for a Hummer? The reason was obvious: it was only a matter of months, before I even graduated, in fact, that I would have more personal net worth than every other student at St. V combined as the result of a $90 million shoe contract with Nike. Was the vehicle excessive, with its bank of three televisions? Maybe. Probably. Of course it was. So were the BMWs parked in the St. V lot, belonging to fellow students. Nobody ever questioned those.

It created a perfect situation for the major national media that was now following the team. The *Los Angeles Times* had crucified us when we had been on the West Coast, then continued to follow our every move on the court against Mater Dei, as if we were the Los Angeles Lakers. The *Plain Dealer* had a beat reporter who covered the team regularly, then added another one whose only intention, as far as I could tell, was to dredge up dirt. ESPN drew strong ratings for the games they televised (the first one garnered 1.67 million viewers, the most on ESPN2 since the funeral of Dale Earnhardt two years earlier). Meanwhile Bill Walton and Dick Vitale held on-air debates on the dangers of overexposure in high school. But if we were being overexposed, it was because of them, not us.

It was a *crazy* situation at times. It was an *out-of-hand* situation. When St. V played at the Palestra in Philadelphia, then 76ers coach Larry Brown had been there, and so had Allen Iverson. But like I said, I was able to shut everything out, keep my focus on school, still doing my homework out of guilt and knowing if I at least did that, I could get a C in the course. I also focused on the dream that, after eight years, we now could actually touch. Because none of this was pressure. Pressure was being born without a father to a mother who was sixteen. Pressure was watching the house that had belonged to the family get condemned by the city and torn down, leaving my mother and me with no place to live. Pressure was staying up half the night worrying if my mom was okay. Pressure was moving from place to place and from school to school. Hummer Hysteria was no kind of pressure to me.

As the athletic association investigation dragged on and on, we kept to our schedule. We continued to try to hold on to our number-one ranking in *USA Today*. Mentor: 92–56, to give us a record of 11 and 0. R. J. Reynolds from North Carolina: 86–56, to give us a record of 12 and 0. Still number one. Still playing well despite all the distractions. Then came the beautiful night that put those distractions into perspective and out of our minds.

It was known as Senior Night, and it was the moment when we seniors were singled out in front of our home fans. Before the game, each senior would walk out to center court with his closest relatives and be introduced to the crowd. We wanted Senior Night to be held at the gym of St. V. With its yellowed floor and bench-style seats, that was where we felt the most comfortable.

We liked the old-fashioned scoreboard that simply read "Home" on one side and "Visitors" on the other. We liked the modest cinder block of Coach Dru's office, where, surrounding a shoddy light switch, he had posted laminated proverbs in little squares. Proverbs 15:1: *A gentle answer turns away wrath, but a harsh word stirs up anger.* Proverbs 27:1: *Do not boast about tomorrow, for you do not know what a day may bring forth.* The simplicity of the St. V gym made it feel forgiving. It *was* the essence of high school basketball. It brought us back to our roots, helped to ground us in the humility that Coach Dru had preached and we as seniors had finally accepted.

The feeling of family was thick and pungent as each senior was introduced to the jam-packed crowd. Sian was the first member of the Fab Five to walk onto the court, arm in arm with his parents. Little Dru went next with his parents and his nephew, so happy and proud he even smiled. Willie was next with his mother and brother, followed by Romeo with his mother and uncle. Then it was my turn.

My mom wasn't there when the ceremony began. She was late for a good reason, handling the necessary paperwork required by the insurance company and the police because of an accident I had had with the Hummer. Luckily I had other family with me. When I walked out on the floor, I was far from alone. On one side of me were Romeo and Willie, on the other Sian and Little Dru. We were one that night. We swayed back and forth in our own unbreakable circle, our unbreakable bond. At this moment, I realized that whatever the Fab Five had accomplished on the court, and might still accomplish, was nothing compared to what we'd accomplished off of it.

All the members of the Fab Five started that night. We beat Walsh Jesuit 98–46 to push our record to 13 and 0. It meant that we would retain the number-one ranking and still have a shot at the national championship. Senior Night was perfect. Too perfect.

II.

On January 25, 2003, I went to a clothing store called Next in Shaker Heights, an upscale suburb of Cleveland. While I was there, a person associated with the store offered me two so-called throwback jerseys. One was of former Baltimore Bullets' basketball star Wes Unseld, the other of former Chicago Bears' phenom Gale Sayers. When I was asked to pose for pictures to be displayed in the store, I said yes. I did not ask for the jerseys. I did not demand them in return for the pictures. I accepted them for what they were, as gifts. I did not try to take advantage of my status as a well-known high school basketball player. I did not go into Next thinking to myself, Hey, I'm LeBron James. What can I get out of these guys? I will say this about those jerseys—they were cool. I was glad to have them.

I thought nothing more about it, until the athletic association learned bits and pieces of what happened as the result of a newspaper story in the *Plain Dealer* on January 30, and once again went on the attack against me and my team. After an investigation that took exactly one day, the athletic association issued its ruling on January 31: I had violated its bylaws on amateurism by capitalizing on my athletic fame by receiving the gifts, which had been priced at around $850 (although I did not know the value when I received them). The maximum amount of a gift allowed by the athletic association was $100. The investigation had largely been conducted by Clair Muscaro, who'd been athletic association commissioner for the past thirteen years, still with a perfect plume of white hair at seventy. The punishment—I was declared ineligible for the rest of the season. It was one of the worst days of my life.

Muscaro at one point said he found out about the incident on January 27 and started his investigation then, which would mean it took five days instead of just one. But a sworn affidavit from Muscaro himself said he did not find out until January 30, and that the source of his discovery was the *Plain Dealer* story. I didn't even know such a rule could be interpreted the way it was. If I did, would I have been that stupid? Of course not. Would I have put my team in jeopardy like that? Of course not. If I wanted to capitalize on my athletic fame, would I have done it for $850 when I could have done it for millions? Like I said over and over at the time and maintain to this day—they were gifts. Once I heard there were questions over them, I returned them. I did nothing wrong.

I could not believe how harsh the penalty could be for something so inconsequential. It was clear to me, as to the other members of the Fab Five and to Coach Dru, that the athletic association was simply gunning for St. V. It felt we had become too big and were getting far too much exposure, and I was having too many moments on SportsCenter. To us, it seemed that the athletic association, in particular Muscaro, had decided we had to be put in our place. When the loan my mom took out for the Hummer did check out after a lengthy investigation, it seemed obvious that the athletic association and

Muscaro went searching for something else. It also seemed obvious that the athletic association had been getting complaints about us from other high schools. Part of it was competitive jealousy. Muscaro himself now acknowledges that St. V was a "very high-profile program and you had a lot of parents and coaches from other schools and kids saying that [this] isn't right. . . . There may have been some petty jealousy on what they were doing." But part of it, I believe, was the specter of a predominantly white Catholic school fielding a starting five in basketball that was four-fifths African American. How had we gotten there? Why were we there? Was it simply jealousy, or was there some racism mixed in? You be the judge.

When I first learned of the suspension, I literally couldn't think. I couldn't shake the feeling that I had somehow betrayed the other members of the Fab Five. I went to practice, forced to sit on the sidelines, crying the whole time. I knew my team would need me at some point. All I wanted was to be there for them, and now I couldn't be. Little Dru and Sian and Willie and Romeo—they had gone into the season with the dream of winning a national championship. Now I had potentially ruined it. Which is why the tears poured down. Which is why the emotions ran over me.

For some reason I am not quite sure of, I began to think of those maps of the United States I had seen in elementary school that never showed Akron. The Fab Five, in our own way, had put Akron on the map, created an excitement perhaps unparalleled in the sports history of the city, an excitement Akron deserved and needed. It was our honor to do that. I couldn't help but feel that certain parts of Akron and Ohio, beyond the racial issues that had first greeted us, had turned against us. They resented us, maybe even hated us.

Sian often felt like the Russell Crowe character in *Gladiator* when he played, going into a den of bloodthirsty spectators instead of a basketball arena—the jealousy of the opposing crowd, the open hostility of whites at many away games whose clear message was "go back where you came from."

Little Dru found the atmosphere mystifying at certain venues, fans who were grown adults with mouths as foul as drunken sailors openly attacking a group of teenagers. He knew that many people felt we were overconfident and arrogant and spoiled, and there certainly had been ample evidence of that junior year, but Little Dru never thought it would reach this level of animosity. "We were just guys playing basketball," he said later. "We never thought it would come to any of that."

I realized I had no privacy anymore. The now-infamous Hummer was being filmed by the media in the school parking lot as if it was a stolen vehicle. When I went to the store and received the jerseys as gifts, somebody obviously leaked it to the *Plain Dealer*, trying to portray what happened in as negative a light as possible. When I went to the movies with my friends, my very presence caused a scene. The attention, at least the positive attention, was intoxicating. I am not going to deny that. But part of me just hungered to be a regular high school kid. I knew I couldn't be that anymore. Celebrity as an eighteen-year-old? Believe me, it wasn't worth it.

I was miserable over the ruling, racked with shame and disappointment and anger, until Coach Dru, wise and humble as always, pointed out a simple truth: "If this is the worst thing that happens to you in your life, you will have lived a pretty good life." The more I thought about that, the more true it seemed. Looking back on it, I see it as some of the best advice I've ever received. It helped put the controversy into perspective, helped to take away my pain and guilt, especially when he also told me this:

"You know I'm gonna make sure I prepare the team the right way to go out and play the game of basketball while you're not here."

The other members of the Fab Five reacted the same way. As my brother, Little Dru felt hurt that I was being attacked by the athletic association and Commissioner Muscaro. Sian felt angry as well, and also cheated. Romeo was at his outraged best: "This was some bullshit. The OHSAA guy, whatever the fuck his name was, had a hard-on for Bron. He was going to try to find something. He was going to dig deep enough until he got something, and he finally did."

Nobody felt sorry for themselves. Nobody gave up on either the season or the dream. In the locker room (where I wasn't allowed) just before the practice where I broke down in tears, my absence was apparently discussed for maybe a minute. It was followed by the realization that there was still a game to be played. "Look around," said Coach Dru. "This is who we are. This is who we can trust. We need to embrace each other and be there for one another, and if we do that, then we'll make it through this." My brothers heard the whispers that they were no good without me, wouldn't be able to do a thing without me, would *lose* without me. To Little Dru, those were just a rallying cry. He saw the upcoming game against McKinley Senior High School, from neighboring Canton, as a perfect occasion to prove just how good a team they could be without me.

There is no doubt that Little Dru and Romeo, had they gone somewhere else, could have both averaged 25 to 30 points a game. They ceded to me the role of major scorer, for the betterment of the team.

They never complained, in part because I dished off to them as much as I could when they were open: I could have gone for 50 every night, but that's not basketball, at least it's not basketball the way I had learned it. But they had ego. They had pride. Whenever there was an article in the *Akron Beacon Journal* or the *Plain Dealer*, I was almost always in the headline, even when I didn't play very well, or in the case of the suspension, wasn't playing at all. Perhaps the most difficult challenge Coach Dru faced all season was getting the team to understand that it wasn't all about me: the other players had a role, a significant one. One of the nicest letters Coach Dru ever received came from a fellow coach in Ohio who wrote, "I've been coaching a lot of years, and what I saw was not a great player but a great team." The newspaper coverage still left the other players deflated, as if they were nonexistent.

The McKinley game gave them a chance to show they weren't just feeding off my success, but were major talents in their own right. In three years of high school, Little Dru had never seen his name in any of the college recruiting books. He was finally mentioned as a senior, and scouts saw him as a growing player who was getting better, but there was still scant recognition even though he'd grown to five-ten. One book said he had the caliber to be a Division III player. He got no letters from colleges and no interest. He only used it as added fuel, much like playing Canton McKinley without me.

"We weren't about to just lay down," was the way Little Dru later put it. Willie also saw it as an opportunity to prove something, and typical of Willie, he felt it was crucial to win so I wouldn't feel let down. It was always his impulse to think of others first.

Canton McKinley had the richest athletic tradition of any school in Ohio. Their team was young and gritty, with a record of 10 and 4. They saw opportunity in my absence. They thought they could win; maybe I thought they could too. The Fab Five's dream pivoted on this game, the irony cruel and bitter: I wouldn't even be a part of it. It was up to my brothers now.

III.

I am nervous. God, I am nervous. It is hard for me to sit still on the sidelines, but my fears are groundless. The General has taken over; his charges are carrying out his commands. Hey, don't you need me out there? Don't you even miss me a little? It doesn't seem like it.

Little Dru is hot. So is teammate Corey Jones. He hits two quick baskets at the beginning of the first quarter to give St. V a 5–2 lead, then expands it to 12–4 with a 3-pointer. McKinley's Pat Papacostas answers with a basket to make it 12–6, but Little Dru lets it fly from downtown with that patented balloon, St. V 15–6 with 1:36 left to play in the quarter. I haven't seen Little Dru in the zone like this since the state championship freshman year when he hit those seven 3s in a row. It's not simply the way he's shooting. It's the way he is running the floor, with complete authority and command. Hey, Little Dru, remember me? I guess not.

For all my fear, there's nothing to fear. Once Little Dru hits that 3, the game has the makings of a blowout. I can rest easy now. I can relax.

But I admit it—there is something pesky about Canton McKinley, like a little kid in a fight who doesn't know when to give up. They close the lead to 5 with less than a minute left on two quick baskets, 15–10. Willie scores from inside off a crisp bullet from Little Dru: 17–10 St. V. McKinley's Stan Hall scores the final basket of the period off an offensive rebound: 17–12 St. V.

It's a healthy lead after just a quarter of play. Yet I'm getting nervous again; Romeo concerns me because he has had the flu all week and he's playing like it, flat and lethargic.

As long as Little Dru continues the way he is, there are no worries. He's giving a clinic out there, a performance of true beauty. His father has to be proud. Dambrot would be proud. I am proud. McKinley closes to 17–15 to begin the second quarter. Little Dru makes a runner high off the glass on the right side. McKinley scores on a basket by Papacostas to make it 19–17. Little Dru goes to the foul line and makes both free throws.

With just over 4 minutes left in the period, McKinley scores two baskets to once again close the lead to 2: 23–21 St. V. Little Dru goes the virtual length of the court all the way to the hole: 25–21 St. V. He steals on the next possession and is fouled. He makes a free throw. St. V 26–21. He follows with a 3 from the right side for his fifteenth point. St. V 29–21.

With less than a minute left, Willie once again gets into the flow, catching an air ball from the corner and converting it into a layup. It expands the lead to 13, 36–23. Papacostas returns with a 3-pointer just before the buzzer to reduce the lead to 10, 36–26 St. V at halftime.

With Little Dru so deep in the zone, it's been a great half. A double-digit lead is a double-digit lead. Nobody can complain about it, except for the General, which is why he is the General. He is worried about Romeo. He knows that Romeo feels lousy. He knows that Romeo still isn't over the flu yet, which is why he has only 5 points and just hasn't been strong to the hoop; he feels so sick he's been getting the dry heaves during time-outs. Little Dru also knows this is basketball, where 10-point leads can evaporate. There is still something tenacious about Canton McKinley, still the little kid who won't quit no matter how outmanned.

So Little Dru buttonholes Romeo during halftime in the locker room. He isn't angry or belligerent, just straight to the point when he sees something that is bothering him.

"Hey, you're going to have to suck it up," he says to Romeo. "I need you. I need you to come on. So come on."

Romeo listens. He knows Little Dru well enough at this point to realize that Little Dru isn't trying to be a jerk, just tough and serious in the heat of what is still a game that can be won or lost. He believes that Romeo can do better. But does Romeo believe that he can do better? Will those words from the General make any difference?

The answer comes early in the third quarter, with St. V up 36–28. Romeo gets the ball and slashes in the paint to the hoop with an energy that was nowhere to be seen in the first half. Romeo repeats the answer a few minutes later when he scores on a nice tip-in. Soon after he grabs a rebound, is fouled, and makes both free throws. At the buzzer, he gives the most resounding answer yet when he goes high to tap the ball in off his own offensive rebound to push St. V to a 12-point lead. Of all the words that Little Dru has said to us over the years, of all the correction and criticism, what he said to Romeo may have been the most important.

Thanks to the night-and-day play of Romeo, the fourth quarter is fine. He drives in the paint, then kisses the ball off the glass so soft and light. He makes a turnaround jumper from fifteen feet off a feed by Sian. He makes a layup off a dish from Little Dru, a 5-point first half complemented by 16 in the second. Our lead hovers in the double digits, 60–50 with 58 seconds left. I'm still having trouble sitting still. But the game has been put away now. Everybody knows it.

McKinley scores to make it 60–52 with 52 seconds left. So what? There's not possibly enough time left. McKinley intercepts a pass, and Hall pulls up for a ten-footer. With 37 seconds left, 60–54. McKinley is fouled. Sean Weatherspoon goes to the line, converting both free throws. With 24 seconds left, 60–56.

McKinley immediately fouls. Corey Jones makes both free throws: 62–56 with 21 seconds left. Now it is over. It has to be. What could happen?

McKinley's Papacostas gets the ball and just heaves it from the left side. It's a desperation Hail-Mary you-got-to-be-kidding there's-no-way forget-about-it get-a-grip 3-pointer.

It goes.

Seven seconds left, 62–59 St. V.

The ball is inbounded to Corey Jones, who is immediately fouled. He makes the first. He misses the second. But it's 63–59 now. Six seconds left. Jones's free throw has iced it. I know that. But if I know it, why am I still so nervous?

The ball is fed to Papacostas. He puts up another Hail-Mary you-got-to-be-kidding not-in-your-life 3-point bomb.

It goes.

St. V 63–62.

Followed by the most beautiful sound I think I have ever heard in a basketball game. The buzzer. We are still undefeated. Still with the dream to be dreamed. And I'm not playing.

14.

Back to the Future

I.

I wanted to play basketball on a court, not in a court of law. Courts have better things to do, and I knew that, but I felt I had no choice. The punishment did not fit the infraction because there was no infraction. I huddled with my mom. We discussed it. It was clear to her, as it was to me, that simply caving in violated every principle that I stood for. A right is a right and a wrong is a wrong, and this was an egregious wrong. If I was guilty of anything, it was bad judgment; although many refused to believe it then, I was still a teenager when the flap over the jerseys unfolded. That meant I was going to make mistakes. That meant I was going to do things I might later regret.

The exposure I had gotten was arguably the most ever received by a high school athlete. I was maintaining an honors average for the current grading period, roughly a point above my usual average. I continued to keep grounded in the season, in large part because the rest of the Fab Five wouldn't allow me to either get a big head or wallow in self-pity. When the incident with the Hummer resulted in the athletic association's investigation, they joked about it and made light of it, refused to let either me or themselves be dragged down by it. "Why you trying to ruin our season?" they asked me. All I could do was laugh, exactly what I needed.

They always kept me grounded, had no stars in their eyes about me like so many others did. Their attitude was, "You're still LeBron James. Don't put on any airs with us, we know who you are." They never glorified me. They understood I was the best player on the team if we needed a point, but I still needed them to get the ball to me. They were adamant that this *was* a team, and they expressed that as well: "You can't do this without us, and we can't do it without you."

II.

The athletic association and St. V had been at odds with each other for four years. After the semifinals freshman year, Coach Dru had walked off the court, saying, "We beat eight," meaning that we had not only beaten the five players of our opponent on the court, but the three referees calling the game. It was a mild reference, but an official of the athletic association heard it and said, "We don't make those kind of comments here." The next day of the finals, right before St. V was about to warm up at the Value City Arena, Coach Dru was called into a meeting room. "This isn't the kind of behavior we want here," Coach Dru remembers Muscaro saying, further claiming that there were reports that Coach Dru had come off the court cursing the referees. "I did make the statement that 'we beat eight,'" Coach Dru replied. "If I need to apologize for making that statement, I will. But you're not going to tell me I came off the court cursing." Anybody who knew Coach Dru also knew that he never used obscenities. The meeting seemed silly and petty. That same year the athletic association questioned whether we had illegally recruited a player named Aly Samabaly. It was true that he had come from France where he had been living with his sister. It was also true that his parents had been killed in Somalia, where he was originally from. According to St. V headmaster Rathz, Samabaly's sister sent him to Akron to go to school: he was taken in by the president of the county board of education in nearby Medina, who had housed many foreign students. The athletic association declared Samabaly eligible at the beginning of the season, according to Rathz, but after St. V moved to a 13-and-0 record, an archrival wrote a letter to the athletic association saying they should investigate. Then came a call from Muscaro, who says he does not recall the incident.

Muscaro also didn't like the schedule we were playing senior year, with its travel all over the country. "It's not what we are about," he said to the *Akron Beacon Journal*. "It should be about hopping in the yellow school bus and going 30 or 45 miles to play in a gym and then coming home again." He felt I was being exploited, and there is no doubt that promoters arranged the games to make money. The school also received appearance fees. There were plenty who exploited me, but this was not a perfect example. These contests senior year showed the shoe companies that I could sell out arenas all over the country, which only raised the bidding. Plus we had our dream, with no way of accomplishing it by taking a yellow school bus. There was no competition left for us in Ohio. "Clair cannot look me in the eye and tell me to my face that I exploited LeBron James or my players," Coach Dru angrily told the newspaper in response to Muscaro's comments. "If Clair thinks this is about money, he is fooling himself. This [is] about a chance for a group of kids to realize a dream that was years in the making." There was Hummergate during my senior year, and now I had been declared ineligible because of receiving two jerseys, largely on the basis of a 135-word article in the *Plain Dealer*. "It was a witch hunt," Rathz concluded. "It was a classic witch hunt from my point of view. They wanted to get [LeBron] and get the school."

I had grown to love St. V after that first period of transition. It wasn't just the success in basketball. Because of the academics, I had gone from being two years below grade level when I started to being on a college prep track. I even suffered through Spanish. I was popular. But the response from the school to my suspension was disappointing, to say the least.

When Coach Dru went into the office of a St. V official the day after my ineligibility was announced, he remembers receiving a shocking response.

"Well, Dru, we're going to support the ruling of the Ohio High School Athletic Association."

"What? You guys really don't know what you're doing here."

"The board has met, and our position is that we're basically going to support this decision that LeBron is going to be ineligible."

"You're not going to side with LeBron and his family?"

"No."

"You're making a big mistake. All the good that has been done because of LeBron James for this school, and you're gonna run from him when he needs you most?"

The attitude of the school, according to Rathz, was, "We weren't being accused of anything. He was." So the initial reaction was, "Let's sit back" as lawyers for both me and the athletic association sorted it out.

The same day I found out I had been declared ineligible, I had the hope that if I communicated with Commissioner Muscaro in an honest way, the matter would be put into the proper perspective. So I wrote him a letter coming from the place I knew best, my own heart.

I want to start by apologizing for this and any other recent controversy involving me. As you might imagine, there are as many minuses as there are pluses associated with having become something of a celebrity, and I have been forced to make some very important adjustments in my personal life and lifestyle because of it.

I readily acknowledged visiting the store and accepting the jerseys, but also pointed out I had no knowledge of their value since no price tags were attached. I reiterated that I returned them to the store. I ended the letter this way:

Commissioner Muscaro, I have worked long and hard at realizing two dreams. Being a good student and an exceptional athlete. Basketball is my life. My senior year is

> very, very important to me and I want to complete it with
> honor and distinction.

I hoped the letter would make a difference, that it would give Muscaro some sense of what I had been dealing with for two years. I hoped that he would see the lack of evil intent in my actions. I hoped and I hoped. It did no good. Instead, the athletic association later tried to use the letter against me because I said that I had been offered the jerseys as "congratulations for my academic and *athletic* achievements."

Muscaro denies there was any vendetta against either St. V or me. "I have no personal vendetta against LeBron James," he now says. Steven Craig, who as counsel to the athletic association dealt with Muscaro extensively, says the notion of him holding a vendetta is simply untrue. "I really don't think there is that bone in his body. I don't think there is an ounce of that." Muscaro is adamant he has "no regrets over the decision that I made. When I look back, the decision I made based on the information I had, I did the right thing." He says he talked to someone at the store when the incident took place but now says he "doesn't know" if it was the person who actually gave me the jerseys. It wasn't.

His name was Joe Hathorn, and he supplied a sworn affidavit. Had Muscaro spoken to him or to me, he would have learned that Hathorn had been a friend and mentor for the past two years. He would have learned that Hathorn was a trustee of Project: LEARN, a nonprofit organization dedicated to improving adult literacy. He would have learned that Hathorn stressed the importance of my academic performance. He would have learned that Hathorn had discovered that I had been designated an honor student at St. V for the grading period. He would have learned that Hathorn told me he was proud of my making the honor roll and gave me a bag containing the two jerseys after removing the price tags. He would have learned my response was, "You don't have to do that, but thank you. I am glad somebody recognizes that I am a good student." Yes, he probably would also have learned that when asked to pose for pictures that could be put up on the wall of the store, I willingly did so. But the suspension stood, which is why I saw court as the only recourse.

So I once again engaged an attorney named Frederick Nance from the Cleveland firm of Squire, Sanders & Dempsey, who had just represented my mother and me in the investigation of the Hummer. On February 4, two days after St. V's win against Canton McKinley, Nance filed a motion for a temporary restraining order and preliminary injunction on my behalf to prevent the athletic association from revoking my eligibility. The ruling by Commissioner Muscaro, according to the brief we filed on behalf of the motion, had been "arbitrary, unreasonable, capricious and oppressive." The brief further stated that Muscaro served as "investigator, prosecutor, judge and jury in what can only be considered an ill-advised and ill-motivated decision." I didn't need legal knowledge to understand the thrust of that statement.

As I saw it this *was* a witch hunt. This was a one-man posse's attempt to humiliate me, subject me to ridicule, rip open rumors that I was corrupt, and ruin a dream. Those are strong words, I know, and so many years after what happened, perhaps I should just let it go. Perhaps I should let bygones be bygones, as I usually do. Perhaps I shouldn't hold a grudge. But this was an injustice, and a hard lesson on the ways of the adult world. I was learning that adults will create scapegoats to satisfy their unwarranted need for revenge, act in a way that isn't fair or for the greater good but only suits their own vindictiveness in trying to destroy someone. I can never forget that lesson.

Muscaro now says he is "extremely proud" of what I have accomplished since turning pro for the community of Akron, which includes raising over $200,000 a year for the local YMCA and the Akron Urban League; refurbishing numerous basketball courts and rec centers; supporting the King James Shooting Stars Classic travel team tournament in Akron with a donation of over $100,000 every year; and bringing the LeBron James Skills Academy to the University of Akron, with seventy-five of the best basketball players in the country in attendance along with coaches from such schools as Duke University, the University of North Carolina, UCLA, and the University of Connecticut. Those are kind words from the commissioner and I appreciate them. But it's too little, too late.

The brief filed on behalf of the motion was a legal document, so it contained its fair share of legalese. But it contained its fair share of what we were convinced were incontrovertible facts. Muscaro called St. V several times in an effort to reach me, since it is standard in investigations by the athletic association to go through the school. After being told by school officials that I did not want to talk to him because I had legal representation, he never tried to contact me directly. "If someone says they don't want to talk to me, then I have to go with what I have to make a decision," Muscaro now says.

According to our brief, no one from the athletic association, despite dealing with my attorney just a few days earlier over the Hummer, made any attempt to reach him to see if a meeting with me could be set up. Counsel for the athletic association did in fact contact Nance, roughly five minutes before the decision to declare my ineligibility was made public. Instead, Muscaro and the athletic association issued their one-day verdict without ever talking to me, without having more than a cursory conversation with my attorney to notify him of the decision, without talking to the person who had handed me the jerseys.

Muscaro, as part of his investigation, did speak to the person at the store who was quoted in the *Plain Dealer* story, Derrick Craig. Craig told him I had received the jerseys, but once again, he was not the one who had actually given them to me. Which meant that Muscaro had yet to find out the exact circumstances under which they had been presented. The athletic association, in their own brief, never specifically stated that Craig was the one who had given me the jerseys.

Muscaro also contacted Robert Rosenthal, a principal of the store. In a sworn affidavit, Rosenthal said he and Muscaro spoke on January 31. According to the affidavit, he told the commissioner he wanted to help, but would need to conduct a thorough investigation of the employees who had been at the store on the day in question to be as accurate as possible. Muscaro said he already had a statement from Craig, but Rosenthal told him that media reports of Craig's participation might be incorrect, according to the affidavit, and that the investigation would be finished by 4:00 or 5:00 p.m. As our brief emphatically asserted, Muscaro simply decided not to wait for the results of the investigation and issued his ruling at 3:15 p.m.

The suspension was meant to punish me for trying to capitalize on my celebrity as an athlete. But, as the brief explained succinctly, it was in fact other people, all adults, who were trying to capitalize on my celebrity. "Newspapers and magazines have capitalized on LeBron's fame, flush with the knowledge that LeBron makes good copy. Le-Bron's own school has increased ticket prices, moved to a larger venue, scheduled games in far-flung locations. . . . By all accounts, LeBron's celebrity is a valuable commodity. For his part, LeBron has tried scrupulously to comply with [athletic association] regulations and has signed no contract that gives him any compensation for his notoriety." I could have made such a deal with Adidas, or Nike, or Reebok. I could have easily walked away from my high school career, put an end to the autograph seekers begging me to sign something so they could then sell it on eBay, put an end to the members of the media climbing over themselves either trying to interview me or just plain trying to write viciously about me, put an end to it all.

In the brief filed by the athletic association and Commissioner Muscaro, they opined as much, as if it was pointless for me to continue to play basketball at St. V anyway, given what awaited me. They argued that the suspension would cause me no "irreparable harm," the standard for granting a temporary restraining order. "[LeBron James's] prospects with the NBA are well known and will not be adversely affected by the loss of his amateur status. Further, the loss of his amateur status presumably allows [James] to pursue lucrative endorsement contracts, and various other business opportunities."

They failed to see the irreparable harm if I could no longer play with my brothers, if I could no longer help them pursue our dream. Irreparable harm had to do with commitment and love and loyalty.

We had come so far. We had waited so long. We had seen the dream fall from our fingers because of our behavior junior year. And we had regained a grasp on it because of our resolve as seniors. We were close and getting closer, still ranked number one, when Muscaro swooped in with what the brief described as his "Kafkaesque determination" that I was the one who had capitalized on my athletic fame. Huh? What about ESPN, with its boffo ratings? What about *Sports Illustrated*, with its splashy cover? What about the *New York Times*? What about the *Los Angeles Times*? What about the *Plain Dealer*? What about the *Akron Beacon Journal*? What about the national networks? What about the local networks? What about the morality of all these different entities in pumping me up to the size of a Thanksgiving Day Parade float? Did it go to my head? Of course it went to my head. I was a teenager.

From my perspective and the perspective of my lawyer, Muscaro clearly wanted to put an end to what he perceived as the LeBron James train. He thought that the controversy over the Hummer would accomplish that. It didn't work; four days later Muscaro seized on the jerseys as evidence that I was no longer an amateur athlete but an athlete looking to see what I could obtain. "The circumstances of the public pressures Muscaro must have felt from finding no violation regarding the Hummer purchase must have impacted the undeniable rush to judgment in this instance," the brief stated. "The two events, separated by a mere four days, obviously impacted Muscaro's judgment."

That's what I felt. That's what my lawyer felt. But would a judge find any merit in the facts and arguments we set forth? As wrenching as it was to accept, was my season actually over? Would adults, whatever the motivation, win out?

On February 5, common pleas judge James R. Williams issued his ruling at a hearing in his Summit County courtroom. The document he issued was a page and a half, minuscule compared to the nearly

100 pages of court documents that had been submitted by both sides. You had to navigate through eleven lines of pure legalese to get to whether I was back in or still out, and there it finally was in black and white: "It clearly appears that plaintiff will suffer immediate and irreparable injury unless a temporary restraining order issues."

Then you had to wade through twelve more lines to get to the best part: "LeBron James' eligibility is restored as of this day, February 5, 2003, and he can begin practicing with the team."

There were two setbacks—he ordered that I be ineligible for an additional game, to be chosen by St. V. He also ordered that the forfeit of our game against Buchtel, mandated by the athletic association, be upheld (we had beaten them by 11). It was a decision I could live with. So could my attorney and the other members of the Fab Five and Coach Dru and my mother. She gave a statement in which she expressed the hope that I would ultimately be able to "focus entirely on schoolwork, basketball and friends, just like any other teenager." Even I knew those days had come and gone.

At the hearing was a flock of reporters, including ones from *USA Today* and the *New York Times*. Courthouse regulars noted that the media interest surrounding it wasn't the most they'd ever seen. Eleven years earlier, a man in Williams's courtroom had pleaded guilty to murder and drew a larger crowd.

His name was Jeffrey Dahmer.

As for St. V, the executive board of trustees did finally come out in support of me. "Our support of LeBron is because of who he is," said trustees' chairman James Burdon. "He's a member of the school community here. In his years as a student at St. V-M, he has excelled academically and socially, as well as athletically. As part of our school community, he deserves our wholehearted support." This statement came before Judge Williams's ruling, which according to my math, meant they took about a week to do something. The words of Chairman Burdon were comforting, but St. V should have been behind me from the very beginning, and it hurt terribly when the school chose another path. Belatedly backing me was just a smoke screen for their initial instinct of wait and see.

III.

Coach Dru told people that the worst thing an opponent could do going into a big game was anger me. He said that I liked the "big stage," and I did like the big stage. I also liked showing fans, whether they loved me or hated me, that nothing could suppress me. The first game after my reinstatement was in Trenton in the Prime Time Shootout against Los Angeles-based Westchester High. We were still ranked number one by *USA Today*, which did not penalize us for the forfeit. Westchester came in ranked seventh in the country by *USA Today*, and they had a great player in six-eight Trevor Ariza, who went on to UCLA and is now with the Lakers. Scalpers got as much as $2,500 a ticket. There were nearly 140 members of the media there, including ones from Japan and the *New Yorker*.

Word travels fast in basketball circles, sometimes inadvertently. When I got suspended, Ariza's mother was at a Lakers game against the Washington Wizards. She apparently started talking to the wife of someone who was affiliated with the NBA. "This guy LeBron's suspended.

Good," she reportedly said. "Now my son can finally showcase. He's the number one player in the country. He's been better than LeBron all along." The quotes made their way to Maverick Carter, who had continued to stay close to me after his days at St. V. He of course told me. "Coach Dru, they've been talking," I said to him during the pregame warm-up. Coach Dru knew then and there Westchester was in terrible trouble.

I had something to prove, and when I have something to prove, I get excited. Just to be able to put on the St. V uniform again, to run out on the court with my teammates, was more than exciting. I felt giddy. Happy. Exhilarated. The game of basketball never seemed fresher. I was revved up when it began. Sometimes in sports that is a great motivator. But sometimes you get too pumped up, too overanxious, too eager to prove, and you lose your flow. Maybe that's what was happening when Westchester took a quick 6–0 lead. Romeo came back with a basket to make it 6–2, and then I took over. I scored 18 points to give us a 20–14 lead after the first quarter. I had 31 at the half as the lead expanded to 41–24. I finished with a career-high 52, or as many as the entire Westchester team collected in a 78–52 victory that only solidified our number-one ranking.

It was probably the best game of basketball I had ever played in high school. After the game, I stood in front of the media. "Maybe if something else comes up, I'll score 52 again," I said, a reference to the jersey incident. Some thought I was making a little joke, and perhaps I was. Looking back on it, I don't think so. I had been treated with harsh unfairness, retaliating the best way I knew how—on the basketball court.

There must have been something in my eyes during the game,

because Romeo saw it. "I knew it was going to be ugly for Westchester," he said later. After the situation with the Hummer had blown up, I had hit for 50 when we played Mentor, then a career high. And Romeo could feel the same cycle repeating itself here. "Every time something bad happens to LeBron, something bad happens to the next team we play."

The saga of the jerseys had not only improved my game, it had drawn the Fab Five even closer together. Through our adversities, we had grown to depend on each other even more. We were now used to people hating us, resenting us, praying for our failure, infuriated by the dynasty we had created over the past four years. As much as St. V had given to us and we had given to them, we still heard rumblings from some in that community that we didn't belong there, that we weren't worth the controversy that whipped endlessly around us. Seasoned sports columnists just loaded and fired. I don't think there was a team in the country—high school, college, or pro—that had endured as much criticism as we did that year. Ever since I had appeared on the cover of *Sports Illustrated*, we had all become targets. None of us liked it or had had much experience with it, except maybe for Romeo, who would never lose his natural gift for attracting hatred, and had developed a particular philosophy: "Hey, I've been hated my whole life. And it's not going to stop now, so people can hate, let 'em hate."

That atmosphere only fortified us, the sense that at the end of the day, there are really so few you can ever depend on. Trust, such a precious commodity for all of us even when we were kids, became more precious now. As Sian said, "We all we got"—we only had ourselves to fall back on, rely on, lean on. We spent more and more time at each others' homes, cut off from anyone else. Sometimes we went over to the second-floor apartment of Willie's mother on the east side. She was now drug free and living in Akron in an apartment complex. Some of us were so tall we had to bend over to get inside. Then she gave us a home-cooked meal that we ravenously soaked up— roast beef, macaroni and cheese, corn bread, yams, greens, ice cream and cake for dessert.

We became more and more suspicious of anybody trying to break into our circle. Who are you? Why are you? What do you want? Why do you want it? Maybe it was paranoia, but it was reasonable to assume that every move I made was being tracked by someone.

The best thing about the Fab Five's bond was how much of it went unspoken. That's how well we had gotten to know each other. When I got suspended, it wasn't necessary for Little Dru or Sian or Willie or Romeo to try to console me or say they were sorry. "We knew his heart," was the way Romeo later put it, and when you know someone's heart, as we all did, there was no need to articulate what was pumping inside it. My brothers knew I was hurting, and there was no need to talk about the hurt. Just knowing we were there for each other and would always be there for each other was all the therapy we needed. Just trying to screen out the cyclone of frenzy surrounding us and staying focused was what we gave to each other the most. Maybe it sounds funny, but it was almost as if we truly were one, just like we had been on Senior Night when we came out to center court together. If we were going to remain undefeated and win a national championship, it's the way we would have to be. There was no other choice.

As for Coach Dru, he grappled with whispers that, despite our success, he wasn't up to the task. He went on the Internet, reading the comments attributing that success to his white assistant coaches. But he took it in stride. "Those are the kind of things that as an African American you just deal with," he said later. "It's just part of what comes with the territory." He refused to let it interfere.

With three games left in the season after Westchester, all of our remaining opponents were from Ohio. We beat Zanesville 84–61. We beat Kettering Alter 73–40 in front of a sell-out crowd of 13,409 at the University of Dayton. Per the order issued by Judge Williams, I was ineligible for the last game of the season against Firestone. I had to sit on the sidelines again, and I'm not one to develop insecurity about anything, but as I watched the game unfold, I did begin to think that Little Dru was getting too used to playing without me. He loved being the General, not just the General who distributed the ball to the rest of us and still let us have it when we didn't obey his orders, but the General who liked to shoot and felt liberated. And shoot he did that night in a 90–43 win, with a career-high 31 points that included six 3-pointers and 24 points in the second quarter *alone*. It meant that he had averaged 26 points a game in my absence, so I knew I had to get back out there just in time for the playoffs.

IV.

In the third game of the playoffs, we faced Central-Hower for the district title. We had played Central-Hower before, but never in a situation like this, with so much at stake and their level of talent so high. They were good, very good, with a record of 22 and 1. They knew they were good, and they resented the fact that we were the team that got all the media focus. They had won the city championship among public schools in Akron.

In the district semifinals, they had played Buchtel at the Canton Memorial Field House. The St. V team was in the stands that night, watching as six-seven forward Jeremiah Wood and fellow six-six forward DeJuan Dennis hit for a combined 51 points in defeating the Griffins 83–65. They played with confidence and swagger, and the win put them into the district championship against us. That was incentive enough, but Central-Hower's coach, Dwight Carter, stoked up the volume when he said this to the *Akron Beacon Journal* about our team:

"Earlier in the year, I read where they had to schedule games all over the country because playing the city teams was too boring. When we play them, we just don't represent Central-Hower. We're playing for every public school in Ohio."

Carter then took another swipe, noting that our sneakers came courtesy of outside companies, first Adidas and then Nike:

"We're just a little public school. Our kids buy their own shoes."

Then came the slap:

"I wouldn't be surprised if we beat them."

The game had now become war. "It was like the city of Akron versus St. V," Little Dru observed. No one went into the war with more of a personal grudge than Romeo. He had gone to Central-Hower, and the ending between him and the school had not been pretty. Now

more than ever you could literally feel Romeo's desire to prove himself. Show the Central-Hower players, many of whom he had played
with, that he had made the right decision by leaving. Show that he
belonged at St. V. Canton Memorial Field House was on fire that day
with a sell-out crowd of 5,023 fans in which scalpers got a hundred
bucks for a pair of five-dollar tickets. Some were calling this the true
state championship.

THE TEMPO IS WILD at the beginning, both teams beyond full throttle.
Turnovers. Steals. Shots falling short. Back and forth. Up and down.
Like a DVD in fast-forward. Will anyone score, or is the pace too
ramped up? We like being up-tempo, and we're not going to change.
But it's Central-Hower that scores first, when Jeremiah Wood makes
a nice roll-in off his fingertips. We answer back, still with the engine
open wide. We even kick it up a notch; then we're flying, gliding,
playing the best basketball of our lives. It's 22–15 St. V at the end of
the first quarter. We put on a 21–5 run in the second quarter. It's 43–20
at halftime, Central-Hower is dizzy and punch-drunk.

There is only one sour note in the first half, and that's Romeo.
Eager to perform, he gets into early foul trouble and spends most of
the first two quarters on the bench with only 4 points. It's killing him
to just sit there. He's asking himself, Why now, why of all times, have
I gotten into foul trouble? He sits on that bench and looks into the
faces of the Central-Hower fans. He can see their glee and he knows
what they are thinking—See, he never should have left. See, he's not
as good as he thinks he is. His old friends are there. His ex-girlfriend

is there. He looks into the faces of the St. V fans and he can tell that they are sad and disheartened and feeling for him. The whole thing is messing with his head, messing with it badly.

At halftime Coach Dru comes up to Romeo. He knows he is wounded. He knows how important this game is to him. He tells him, "We're coming back to you." He wants the game to be in full blowout mode, and he knows that Romeo can do that for us. "We're winning without you and so we're going to blow them out with you, so get ready," says Coach Dru at halftime.

Romeo comes back out in the second half. He is playing looser, more freely. He gets a feed for an easy layup for the first basket of the third period. St. V 45–20. He gets a feed from Little Dru and slashes inside to the hoop past Jeremiah Wood. St. V 49–22. He gets another feed from Little Dru to make a thundering dunk. St. V 53–24. He is suddenly in double figures in scoring, with the third quarter still in its infancy. He has scored 6 of the team's first 10 points in the quarter. None of the Central-Hower fans are looking at him with glee now. Not his old friends. Not his ex-girlfriend.

Romeo has awakened. He has arisen. He scores 8 more points before the game is through on the way to the 83–56 blowout that Coach Dru was looking for. He finishes his 14-point second-half flourish with another rattling dunk to give him 18 for the game.

AFTERWARD, COACH DRU told us that our focus was the best he'd seen since we'd played Oak Hill our sophomore year. The victory inspired us only more. Four more wins, and the state championship would be ours. The national championship would be ours. The dream would be ours. First came Tallmadge in the regional semifinal, beaten by 50. Then came Ottawa-Glandorf in the regional finals, beaten by 10. Then came Canton South in the state semifinals in Columbus, beaten by 25. It was down to one.

15.

Shooting Stars

I.

After all we had been through, the twists on the court we'd prepared for, the twists off the court we never could have prepared for, this final game felt so sweet and so bittersweet. Not just a season but our whole lives together reduced to 32 minutes.

After this game, no pact could keep the Fab Five together. I knew I would declare for the NBA draft, and the rest of the Fab Five had their own aspirations. The knot that had so tightly bound me to Little Dru and Sian and Willie and Romeo would soon unravel. The expression of our bond on the basketball court, where each of us always knew where the others were, would disappear.

We still had a grand dream to catch. But during the week of the final four, it was hard to shut out our emotions. Although we had started at different times, we still felt like Shooting Stars, still felt the same exhilaration of playing basketball together when luck and fortune and the grace of God.had brought a bunch of kids from the former Rubber Capital of the World together under Coach Dru. It was as if that ride in the minivan had continued for eight years.

If we felt the bittersweet sweet, so did Coach Dru. His hand had guided us from the beginning; it was he who had driven that minivan all the way to this moment. As he had prepared us for the state semifinals against Canton South, he knew his primary task was to not let sentiment take hold. Even he couldn't help but think that, win or lose in Columbus, this would be the last time he would coach his son, with whom his relationship had flowered senior year. It was a combination of two stubborn personalities finally moving toward the same common point. Little Dru had matured and become less defensive. He still blew up from time to time when he didn't like the way practice was going, but it wasn't aimed in the direction of his father anymore. Coach Dru no longer felt he had to justify his son's presence on the court. He finally realized that Little Dru was a great player, with no need to single him out over and over. He was always going to be a little harder on his son than on the rest of the team—old habits never quite die—but he also allowed him to grow through his mistakes without tearing him up. Because of how he had treated Little Dru in the past, Little Dru inherited the same role for himself. He was merciless on himself, which meant Coach Dru no longer had to be merciless.

When they were in the car together, the discussions now centered on loftier issues than getting beat off the dribble or not taking a charge. Coach Dru knew that his son, to achieve his goal of playing Division

I basketball, had to rise to the next level of team leadership. It was an intangible quality, difficult to address directly, so he just posed a seemingly simple question: "There's a whole bunch of little guys who shoot well, but can they lead a team? Can they be decision makers?"

He let Little Dru ponder that in silence.

Coach Dru realized that in a matter of days, once he relinquished his role as coach of his son, it would be harder to have these conversations. Little Dru might not play Division I, but he was going to play somewhere, and it would be up to another coach to take Little Dru in his hands and craft and shape him. Just as Coach Dru realized it would be the last time he would coach Sian and Willie and Romeo and me. It was easy to get lost in the ending of it all. So Coach Dru did what he knew best—he coached. He made sure we followed the same routines we always followed, that we didn't treat the state championship differently than any other game.

Our opponent was Archbishop Alter from Kettering. We had played them during the regular season, that game a 33-point blowout. Coach Dru, with the memory of Roger Bacon seared into his mind forever, did everything to prevent us from becoming overconfident. He meticulously prepared us for what they might try to change this time, what kind of game plan they might use to better match up against us. He knew, as we knew, there was a national championship at stake; it was a foregone conclusion that *USA Today* would keep us at number one if we won or drop us from the top spot if we lost. He knew, as we knew, it should have been all the incentive we needed.

The night before, I looked for karma. Lying in bed, I wondered about my back. Would it suddenly cramp up like it had the year before? Would there be pain and stiffness? I woke up the day of the game feeling fresh and healthy. Did that mean we should beat Kettering Alter? Of course we should, given our history with them.

We also should have beaten Roger Bacon.

Coach Dru gathered the team in the locker room before the game. He told us to look around and talked about how this would be the last time many of us would ever play together. He talked about the different paths our lives would take because that was the inevitability of life. He talked about what a long ride it had been for some of us, and what a good ride it had been as well. He talked about how you never want things to end, but there's a time and a place where all things must come to an end. Then he said:

"The best way to end this thing is by winning."

He turned to the grease board to go over strategy one more time, but then he stopped.

"Forget all of this stuff. Forget about it. This is all about what's inside here. It's all about heart."

Then he finished.

"Fellas, you just have to go out there and leave everything out on the court."

II.

Something isn't right from the very beginning, and it's not because we're tight. Kettering Alter is a completely different team from the one we destroyed five weeks ago. Their coach, Joe Petrocelli, has put in a game plan that feels like an ambush. He has won the state championship three times with Kettering Alter, most recently two years ago. He has been a state semifinalist five times. With his rounded face and puffy chin and disappearing neck, he looks more like a weary traveling salesman than a basketball coach. His eyes seem almost sad, but in reality they are the eyes of a fox. He has won 691 games and lost only 215 during his thirty-nine-year career. He knows. He just knows.

It's a slowdown strategy that makes the game of basketball painful to watch. It is also making the game painful for us to play, taking away the up-tempo rhythm that is our badge and birthright. Can you believe this? We have a game on our hands before yet another record crowd for a state tournament game, 18,454.

It starts out well enough. I score on a slam dunk off a feed from Little Dru. It's a nice opening statement. St. V 2–0.

Kettering Alter starts slowing things down as soon as they get the ball. They run a minute-plus off the clock until they are called for traveling. We get the ball back. Turnovers are traded, and Kettering Alter plays the same slowdown routine. With 3 minutes gone in the first period, there has still been only one basket. With 4 minutes left, there has still been only one basket. We could fall into deep frustration at the snaillike pace. But we are staying cool. We are staying calm. We are maintaining our composure. The game will come to us. It will eventually come to us. We know that, and we are patient.

With 3:30 left in the quarter, six-five sharpshooting guard Doug Penno, on his way to Miami University of Ohio, hits for a 3-pointer. Kettering Alter 3–2. Romeo comes back with a nice left-hander. St. V

4–3. But Kettering Alter is still in slowdown mode. What's the rush? With a little over 3 minutes left to play, they've had four possessions and made thirty-six passes.

Penno hits a jumper from the left side with 2:53 left. Kettering Alter 5–4.

I come back with a layup off a long feed from Little Dru. St. V 6–5.

Kettering Alter's Jack Hilgeman makes a foul shot. Tied 6–6 with 2:24 left.

I go to the hoop with 1:40 left. St. V 8–6.

I score again but get called for an offensive foul. Still 8–6, with 70 seconds left in the quarter.

Kettering Alter continues their slowdown. Seventy seconds. Sixty seconds. Fifty seconds. Forty seconds. For God's sake, just be a man. Just shoot the thing. They aren't listening to me. They are listening to their coach with that little cherub face of his and his 691 career wins. Thirty seconds. Twenty seconds. Let's play some basketball. Enough of this cowardice.

With 17 seconds left, they lose control of the ball. We finally get it back, and Corey Jones goes for a 3 and misses. For the first time all period, Kettering Alter rushes urgently to get off a shot, as if they have something to do. Hilgeman shoots a jumper . . .

And just narrowly misses as the buzzer sounds to end the first period, 8–6 St. V.

Eight lousy points for a team known for its take-no-prisoners style of play. This can't be happening. It must not be happening. But we are still gathered. There is no bitch-and-moan about the referees in the huddle during time-outs like there was against Roger Bacon. We know what we need to do. We know we need to redirect the flow of the game to our style.

I OPEN THE SECOND PERIOD with a steal and a dunk. St. V 10–6.

Maybe this is the turnaround we are looking for. But Kettering Alter is still trying to kill us softly. Penno misses a short jumper, still shaving more than 2 minutes off the clock.

Kettering Alter's Andy Stichweh goes inside to the hoop. St. V 10–8.

I answer back with a 3-point play on a drive inside through the paint. St. V 13–8.

In a game as slow and low scoring as this one, a 5-point lead might as well be a 15-point one. We feel like there's finally an opening now. We can sense turnaround, and it's about time.

Penno drives baseline for Kettering Alter. St. V 13–10.

Eric Laumann makes a steal for Kettering Alter and hits a bank shot. St. V 13–12.

I am fouled on a jumper and make a foul shot. St. V 14–12.

Kettering Alter's Adam Gill is fouled going backdoor and makes a foul shot. St. V 14–13.

They get the ball back on a turnover. Hilgeman hits off the glass. Kettering Alter 15–14. Which means they are winning, with less than 3 minutes left in the first half. *They are now winning.*

I miss a one-and-one. Gill comes back with a basket inside. Kettering Alter 17–14.

With 26 seconds left, a bad pass from Little Dru is stolen. Penno gets the ball and drives off the dribble. He scores. Kettering Alter 19–14.

THAT'S HOW THE FIRST HALF ENDS, with us down by 5. We have scored only 6 points the second period. We have made only two field goals. We have been outrebounded and outshot. We are trying to keep calm in the locker room, just shut out negative thoughts. But it isn't easy. Willie has a vision of seeing those double zeros on the scoreboard to indicate that time has run out, with St. V on the losing end. He is afraid of getting again that empty feeling in his chest when we lost to Roger Bacon, the worst he had ever felt in his life. He is shocked, surprised, even scared that history will repeat itself. Sian, on the other hand, isn't nervous at all. He knows they are stalling, but he thinks it is a transparent strategy that can't sustain itself. In his mind there is no doubt St. V will win.

Coach Dru is hardly surprised by the game plan. He figured that Petrocelli would in effect try to shorten the game by holding on to the ball for as long as possible, taking away our aggressiveness. What he didn't think is that Kettering Alter would be as good at it as they have been. The refereeing has been bad, in his mind. He cautions us, "Don't let the officials get to you. You can't let them get to your head." He huddles with his coaching staff and realizes that some changes have to be made. Penno, who had 9 points in the first half, needs to be neutralized. I have been guarding him, and I need to score. I can't be chasing Penno all over the court, getting frustrated. Coach Dru makes a defensive switch, decides to put Little Dru on Penno with instructions to go wherever he goes so he doesn't get an open shot, blanket him, act like a second jersey on him. "I don't care if you score a point," he says to his son. "I don't want Penno scoring another point." Romeo has been on the bench for most of the first half after he picked up his second foul. He'll be back on the court now, which should help our press on defense and give us added force on offense.

Then Coach Dru tells the team to stop counting on me to win the game for them. He felt that happened against Roger Bacon, and he feels it may be happening now. What he's really trying to say is that our success has been as a team, not as individual pieces. "There are a whole lot of things going on here, and you have to do your job. Do your job and don't look around in frustration because they're holding the ball and thinking LeBron is going to bail you out. Because right now LeBron can't bail us out because they're holding the ball. We're not getting a chance to shoot it. You have to play defense throughout the whole possession."

I sit and I listen to Coach Dru, and I know he makes sense. I see him in his gray jacket and white turtleneck looking so poised, light-years removed from the tentative man who had taken over with such uncertainty when Dambrot left. He speaks with authority. He speaks with truth. He speaks with sharpness. One player alone cannot win this game.

But I feel a sense of obligation that goes beyond just our senior season. It goes back to when the first members of the Fab Five came out of nowhere to finish ninth in the national AAU tournament. It goes back to eighth grade, when I missed the shot against the SoCal All-Stars. It goes back to the first game against Oak Hill sophomore year, when I missed the shot again. And it goes back to the responsibility I feel toward my brothers to fulfill our dream. Silently, I make a promise in that locker room at the Value City Arena at Ohio State: I will not let us lose.

Just as I know that promises, like dreams, are made to be broken.

III.

Romeo opens the third period by scoring from underneath. Kettering Alter 19–16.

Laumann answers with a wide-open fifteen-footer. Kettering Alter 21–16.

St. V gets the ball back on a steal by Corey Jones. Over to Romeo, who, just as Coach Dru predicted, has come alive. He goes inside. Kettering Alter 21–18.

Kettering Alter takes it back up. There's a steal by Little Dru, who is playing defense just like his father asked him, guarding Penno so tightly Penno can barely breathe. He dishes to me, and I am fouled with three defenders trailing. It's a shooting foul, but I miss both. Kettering Alter 21–18.

They get the ball back and throw it away. It's their third turnover of the quarter, meaning our pressure defense is rattling them.

I go to the hole inside and get the roll off the rim. Kettering Alter 21–20.

There is a change of possession off a block by Romeo. I get the ball and go to the hoop through the paint. St. V 22–21.

Then I block a shot. I race down the court and I can take the shot, and maybe I will. But out of the corner of my eye I see Corey Jones open for a 3. I pass it to him. He hits. St. V 25–21.

We have gone on a 9–0 run. Kettering Alter has turned the ball over five out of their last nine possessions. They are broken now. Little Dru has submerged Penno into silence. Romeo has come alive. Sian is acting like a duty guard on defense. I am finding the open man.

Then Laumann pulls up for a line-drive ten-footer. It goes with 55 seconds left in the quarter. St. V 25–23.

Laumann hits again on a backpedaling five-footer after missing a layup. Tied 25–25.

Little Dru holds the ball for a final shot. He goes to the hoop, then passes off to Romeo with 2 seconds left. It's good. St. V 27–25.

We have played our game in the third quarter. We have outscored Kettering Alter 13–6. We have pressured them into turnovers on defense. Penno hasn't scored a point. But we're still only up by 2. With 8 minutes left.

THE FOURTH PERIOD BEGINS.

I score on a lob from Little Dru that is perfectly timed, like we have been doing it for much of our lives, which we have. St. V 29–25.

Penno just misses on a tip-in, so he's still scoreless in the second half.

I go up for a shot on the return possession and get fouled. I make both. St. V 31–25.

I steal the ball after the free throws. I take two dribbles and pull up for a 3-pointer from the left side with 5:14 left. Good. St. V 34–25.

St. V has scored 7 straight points. Kettering Alter has committed seven turnovers in the second half. St. V hasn't committed a single one. The momentum has completely shifted our way.

Laumann hits a 3-pointer for Kettering Alter, wide open. St. V 34–28.

I take the inbounds pass from Little Dru. Off the glass. St. V 36–28.

Then Sian scores on a tip-in of his own shot. St. V 38–28.

There is 3:37 left, and we're up by 10. It's finished.

Penno makes a great pass inside to Stichweh for an easy layup. St. V 38–30.

Corey Jones answers up the weak side. St. V 40–30.

Willie has only played 5 or 6 minutes because the early tempo of the game has been so slow. But he acts like a coach on the sidelines, dropping to his knees, warning a player on the floor that he needs to get back because a Kettering Alter player is behind him, telling other players to box out and close out, trying to be an extra pair of eyes.

There are 2 minutes left, and now we are slowing it down. But then I see Corey Jones for an uncontested 3 with 1:25 left. I pass it to him and yell "shot," which is what we do when a man is open. It's stupid on my part, ill-advised, because they are the ones chasing us. He misses. Coach Dru calls time-out, and I can tell that he wants to choke me.

"What are you doing?" he asks me.

"My bad," is all I can say.

Kettering Alter gets the ball back. Penno goes for a desperation 3 from way downtown with 1:15 left. He hits it. St. V 40–33.

There is a flurry of back-and-forth possessions: 1:03 left. *Forty-five* seconds left. *Thirty-seven* seconds left. Little Dru misses a one-and-one with *thirty* seconds left. Still 40–33.

Kettering Alter takes the ball upcourt. Bo Keyes goes for a 3-pointer. He misses. But Adam Gill gets the rebound and puts the ball in as he is fouled. St. V 40–35.

He makes the free throw with 22.7 seconds left. St. V 40–36.

A time-out is called, both teams huddling, both coaches deep in the last gasps of strategy. We maintain possession on the inbounds, but then I throw it away and Kettering Alter retrieves it.

They are still alive.

Zach Freshwater goes for a 3 from the left corner to put Kettering Alter within 1. The ball rises off his fingertips with 6.3 seconds left, and there's a certain breathlessness in the air, the all-too familiar slow-motion feeling. It goes and it goes. It hits the rim . . .

And then bounces out to a waiting Romeo.

He is immediately fouled. He goes to the line . . .

He misses.

But I pull in the rebound and send it over to Little Dru. He starts his dribble, and he keeps on dribbling until the clock reveals our destiny.

Zero.

WE RAN OUT onto the court mobbing and hugging each other like the little boys we once were. The first emotion Little Dru felt was relief. He had watched time running out and the score getting tighter and tighter and he felt the pressure and he did not want to come this close and let the game slip away. Then the relief became euphoria. He threw the ball into the air and did a lap around the court, giving fans high fives. He felt like it was Christmas Day when you ran down the stairs and got the gift that you had been asking for over and over. He saw his dad, who was in tears. Little Dru knew his father was proud of the Fab Five, and Little Dru was proud of his father, whatever they had gone through. He knew that his father had been the first one to put a basketball in his hands. It was his father who had truly gotten the Shooting Stars up and running and had treated basketball like he was going back to school, reading all those books, watching all those tapes, attending all those clinics, doing whatever he could to be a better coach. Little Dru now knew that all the hard work had finally culminated in something glorious.

Sian looked over and saw his mother and father and Coach Dru and Carolyn Joyce and his brother L.C. He felt like he was dreaming, but now in a dream that was real with everybody who had been there from the very beginning. He started cutting down the net, realizing there was no one in the world he would rather play basketball with than the other members of the Fab Five, because they were his teammates, because they were his finest friends.

Romeo felt he was in the best place on earth. He believed most people live lives of dreariness and routine, doing their job, going home to their families, not really ever changing anything. But Romeo knew he had changed something, left a mark. He had won a national championship, and no one could ever take that away from him. He also felt the Fab Five had left a mark on Akron. It might not last forever, but at that moment, Akron meant Dru Joyce and Sïan Cotton and Willie McGee and Romeo Travis and LeBron James. It was no longer the city that provoked a first reaction of "Where the hell is that?"

Willie looked into the stands to find his brother Illya, just to thank him for all the opportunities he had made possible—an existence away from the streets of Chicago, a better life in Ohio, a free education at a Catholic school, a million and one things that had all made Willie the man he was rapidly becoming. When Willie played on his first basketball team, it was Illya who had taken him there. When he first went to junior high school, it was Illya who had taken him there. When he first attended St. V and worried about whether he could handle it academically, it was Illya who had been there to reassure him. As the winning of the national championship sunk in, he couldn't help but trace it all back to his brother, a full and perfect circle. Willie found Illya, who was in the aisle in the stands about halfway up. He climbed into the spectator section and ran up the steps and gave Illya a hug that seemed to last for half an hour.

"This is all because of you," he said. "I couldn't have done this if it wasn't for you."

Tears ran down Illya's face.

"I love you. I'm so proud. You just made me the proudest person in the world."

Then he gave Willie words of typical wisdom:

"This is your time now. It's not my time. And you enjoy it. We'll be here. You go and enjoy it with your friends because you've earned it. This is your time."

I too felt the joy of celebration, and I couldn't help but think how all of this had started in fifth grade, that little kernel we never gave up on. A lot of people set goals in life but never fulfill them. They give up on them, let go of their dreams—after all, they are just dreams. But we had not. We had accomplished our goal and dream, and as members of the Fab Five, we had done it in the last game of basketball we would ever play together. It seemed like a story made in heaven to me, something that couldn't possibly have happened except that it did.

We all went through a gamut of emotions, what Willie later described as a mixture of joy and laughter and sadness and tears. It was hard not to go back in time to what I had been through in my life to get here—growing up without a father, moving from place to place, the wail of the police sirens, being worried to death that my mother would never come home and I would be completely alone. It was hard not to think how lucky I had been to have the love of the Walkers and then find a father figure in Coach Dru. It was even harder not to think how lucky I had been to find a family in Little Dru and Sian and Willie and Romeo. It was hard not to think of all the nights we had spent together at Coach Dru's house, destroying his rec room with the knee football we played. It was hard not to think how important it was that we stuck together as one when the black community of Akron accused us of being traitors for not going to public school. It was hard not to think how essential our support to one another had been when we made the transition to a school that at first seemed so alien and different, strangers in a strange land. It was hard not to think about all we had learned about teamwork and focus and respect and the potential disaster that can happen when you lose sight of them. It was hard not to think how we had pulled each other through when it seemed like a world of adults was against us and hated us and wanted us to fail. It was hard not to think about the beauty of dreaming.

But it was also hard not to think that we *would* go our separate ways in just a few months. We would, as Coach Dru had told us before the game, follow different paths. In achieving our dream, another dream, maybe one even more powerful, had been lost. The Fab Five? It was history now, already a memory as we stood at mid-court in the Value City Arena and received our trophy and were hailed as national champions. Which is why, in the tears that we shed, it was impossible to know where the joy ended and the sadness began.

16.

Fab Five

In the basement of my home, four frames have been carefully placed on the farthest wall. The three largest ones catch your eye immediately as you walk down the carpeted steps. One frame contains the jersey I wore in my inaugural appearance with the Cleveland Cavaliers on October 29, 2003, after becoming the first overall pick of the NBA draft straight out of St. V. Another frame contains a signed jersey from Kobe Bryant. The third, laid flat in the frame with the same kind of care, is from Michael Jordan, with the same number 23 that I now wear.

It is the fourth frame that is the most precious to me. It's much smaller than the other ones. Within it is a collage of pictures, ten of them altogether, most of them showing me in various poses playing basketball at St. V. But the photograph at the lower right has the greatest value. It was taken on St. V's graduation day in 2003. There are five of us in it, and we are all wearing caps and gowns of a bright green only appropriate for a high school whose nickname is the Fighting Irish.

I am in the center, with an enormous smile on my face. On one side are Sian and Little Dru. They too are smiling, but in very different ways that seem to reveal their disparate personalities. Sian is laughing, with his cap pulled so far back on his head, it's poised to fall off at any second. Little Dru, with his head tilted to the side, has a smile that is soft and shy. On the other side are Willie and Romeo. Willie's smile is a Willie smile, reflective and a little bit inward. Romeo's grin is big and toothy, a little bit out there, just like Romeo himself.

I love this picture and always will. It reminds me of what the Fab Five did on the basketball court, playing with a purity and joy that I have yet to find in the NBA, with its travel and trades and players moving in and out. I adore the NBA, relish the challenge of it. But it is a business.

I love this picture because it reminds me of the personalities that meshed together as we were transformed from boys into men—the chip on the shoulder and the lion's heart of Little Dru, the take-no-prisoners loyalty of Sian behind the fun-loving and sometimes angry exterior, the mature selflessness of Willie in refusing to simply do what was best for himself, the unpredictable say-anything of Romeo, no matter how much he had grown up.

What affects me the most is not what the picture says about the past, but what it says about the future. The Fab Five never did play a game of basketball again together after winning the national championship. But contrary to my fears, we have endured. What we ultimately brought to the city of Akron cannot be diminished, nor can the pride. It is a place that we cherish, and we all still live in its environs.

We obviously don't see each other as much as we used to. When we do, there is still the same music of laughter and chatter. We sometimes go on trips together during the summer—Las Vegas one year, Mexico another. Whatever my status in the NBA, they still treat me like their brother.

We are, as Sian put it, "friends for life." And what can be more important than that? Nothing that I know of. We remain a family, wherever our paths take us.

We remain the Fab Five.

Afterword

Lee Cotton stopped coaching after St. V won the national championship in 2003. He went on get his Bachelor of Arts degree from the University of Phoenix in 2007 and subsequently a Master of Business Administration from the same institution.

Sian Cotton attended Ohio State on a football scholarship. Redshirted his freshman year, he said he lost his incentive. He began to miss practices. He also stopped going to classes and indulged in excessive partying that he attributed to his own immaturity. He fell out of the coaches' good graces, and spent little time playing over the next two years. He left the school in the spring of 2006. He now attends Walsh University in Ohio, where he played defensive line on the 2008 team and has a year of eligibility left. Now up to 330 pounds, the Detroit Lions, New York Jets, and St. Louis Rams have worked him out, and he hopes to play in the NFL.

Keith Dambrot served as an assistant coach at the University of Akron, a Division I school, for three seasons before being named head coach in 2004. In 2006–7 he coached the team to twenty-six wins, tying a school record. In the 2008–9 season he led the University of Akron to a berth in the NCAA playoffs.

Dru Joyce II was named Coach of the Year by *USA Today* in 2003 after St. Vincent–St. Mary won the national championship. In 2008–9 he led St. V to its second state championship. During his eight seasons there, he has a record of 158 and 42. His teams have won eight sectional championships, six district championships, and four regional championships. He runs the King James Shooting Stars Classic, one of the largest travel team tournaments in the country. More than 550 teams participated in 2008, bringing in $5.4 million to the Greater Akron area. He also helps run the LeBron James King's Academy basketball camp.

Dru Joyce III walked on at the University of Akron and played college basketball there for four seasons. He started ten games at point guard as a freshman in 2003–4 and then was a starter virtually the rest of his career. As a senior in 2007, he set the school's career record for assists with 503. He also joined the 1,000-point scoring list with 1,046. Now six feet tall, he has played pro basketball in Germany the past two seasons in the Bundesliga basketball league with the team Ratiopharm Ulm. In 2007–8 he finished second in the league in assists and led the league in assists in 2008–9. He also played with the Cleveland Cavaliers in the 2008 NBA Summer League.

Illya McGee is now a program manager at Oriana House and was the assistant basketball coach at St. V in 2008–9. Willie and Illya's mother has been drug free for about twelve years after moving to

Akron. Their father, who still lives in Chicago and works at a hotel, has been drug free for close to twelve years as well.

Willie McGee attended Fairmont State University in West Virginia on a football scholarship. He graduated in May 2008 with a bachelor of science degree in information systems. He originally wanted to attend Howard University on a football scholarship, but no money was available. I offered to pay the first year of his tuition, but Willie typically declined. He was the freshman basketball coach at St. V in 2008–9. He is planning this fall to begin a master's program at the University of Akron in sports management.

Romeo Travis played college basketball at the University of Akron for four seasons. He was named Mid-American Conference Player of the Year his senior year in 2006–7, and honorable mention All-American. He was the school's leading scorer in 2006–7 with an average of 14.9 points per game. He set a career record for blocks, with 165, and is the school's seventh leading scorer of all time, with 1,491 points. He played pro basketball in Spain in 2007–8 and in the midst of the season moved to the same team as Little Dru in Germany. He played there the entirety of the 2008–9 season, averaging 13 points and 5 rebounds per game. He also played with the Cavaliers in the NBA Summer League in 2007 and 2008.

"Nobody at nine could have told me I would go to college on a full scholarship," said Romeo. "Nobody at the age of nine could have told me I was going to be a professional basketball player.

"The lesson is that no matter how gloomy the start is, it can always get better."

ACKNOWLEDGMENTS

A book such as *LeBron's Dream Team* is the product of many people and many voices.

First and foremost comes my family, Savannah and our children Bryce Maximus and LeBron Jr. Words are insufficient to describe the joy you have given me. I love all of you very much, and I cannot begin to tell you how full you have made my world.

I would like to thank Sian Cotton; Little Dru Joyce (who isn't so little anymore); his father, Dru Joyce II; Willie McGee; and Romeo Travis for the countless hours they spent in interviews, phone calls, and e-mails to help reconstruct the story of our fantastic journey together. Coach Dru was particularly generous with his time, and it made a lasting difference.

I feel a great debt to those who have supported me so much, not simply during the writing of the book but during my life, with their friendship and guidance and love. These include Coach Dru; the other members of the Fab Five; Eddie Jackson; Frankie Walker Jr. and his parents, Frankie Sr. and Pam; Brandon Weems; Brandon's mother, Brenda, may she rest in peace; and of course my amazing mother, Gloria.

I would like to give a special thank you to my friend and manager Maverick Carter. Maverick, who also is the chief executive officer of LRMR, the marketing and branding company that handles all my business affairs, played an invaluable role in helping to create the vision for *LeBron's Dream Team*. He was also inexhaustible in helping cowriter Buzz Bissinger whenever he had a question, of which he had many, or urgently needed a phone number.

The editor of *LeBron's Dream Team*, Eamon Dolan, did a masterful job. His thoroughness was remarkable, and if there is anyone in the world of publishing who works harder and sleeps less, I don't know who it could possibly be. Thanks also to Eamon's former assistant Laura Stickney, current assistant Nicole Hughes, production editor Noirin Lucas, publicists Sarah Hutson and Caroline Garner, jacket designer Darren Haggar, and interior designer Amanda Dewey. *LeBron's Dream Team* never would have been possible without the support of Ann Godoff, the president and publisher of Penguin Press. Nobody has a better eye for books than Ann does.

The work of the one-and-only literary agent Morton Janklow and general counsel Bennett Ashley of Janklow & Nesbit Associates was instrumental. So was agent Eric Simonoff. So were the efforts of my lawyer Matt Johnson and Buzz's lawyer David Colden.

Many people agreed to be interviewed, but particular appreciation must go out to Lee and Debra Cotton, Keith Dambrot, La'Kisha Lewis,

Dale McGee, Illya McGee, John McGee, Makeba McGee, Harvey Sims, Carolyn Travis, De Shawnda Travis, and Frankie and Pam Walker. At St. V, public relations director Patty Burdon worked tirelessly to supply needed information and compile some of the photographs that you see in the book. I also must thank Barb Wood. Both were at St. V when I was there. Because of them, and many others, the school will always have a special place in my heart. I would be remiss in not singling out Coach Dambrot, who did so much to make me the basketball player that I am today. I even miss his yelling at me.

I give my gratitude to the makers of the film documentary *More Than a Game*, which is similar in theme to the book. Director and producer Kris Belman and producer Harvey Mason Jr. supplied Buzz with material such as interview transcripts and tapes of key games. The rest of the crew, Scott Balcerek, Stephanie DeNatale, Brad Hogan, Richard Kimble, Tom Moser, and Matt Perniciaro, could not have been more accommodating. The same goes for Michele Campbell and Richard Paul of LRMR. And I would be lost without my personal assistant, Randy Mims.

The work of the *Akron Beacon Journal* writers who covered St. V when I was there, Tom Gaffney, David Lee Morgan Jr., Terry Pluto, Tom Reed, and Brian Windhorst, was indispensable, especially in helping to reconstruct some of the games that are depicted in the book. These include the game against Central-Hower during the 1999–2000 season, games against Oak Hill and Buchtel during the 2000–2001 season, games against Amityville and George Junior Republic during the 2001–2 season, and the game against Mater Dei during the 2002–3 season. Morgan's book *LeBron James*, written in 2003, was a valuable resource, in particular in the recounting of a speech given by Coach

Dru before a crucial game. As you can tell from the photographs in *LeBron's Dream Team*, the marvelous work of *Akron Beacon Journal* photographer Phil Masturzo helped to forever memorialize the world of St. V basketball that existed back then. Photography editor Kimberly Barth took time out from her busy schedule to help locate pictures for use in the book.

Finally, I would like to thank Buzz Bissinger for his work and devotion in the creation of *LeBron's Dream Team*. Since Buzz is only five-six, I had trouble finding him sometimes. And he is one serious dude. But I have never met a writer more professional or dedicated, and at this point in my career I have met many of them.